Balkan Melodies
for Classical Guitar

Tanja Mirić

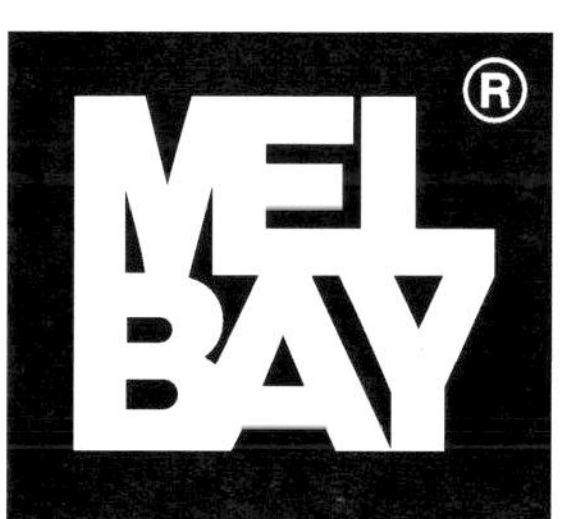

WWW.MELBAY.COM

Preface

The Balkan region boasts of a rich musical culture. In this collection the performer will experience: traditional Bosnian songs adorned with melisma and tremolo, an Italian aria-like song from the coast of Croatia (Dalmatia), Arabic sounding songs from Greece and Turkey, an irregular meter in various songs, the playful effects of minor seconds in a Romanian dance, and lively songs from Slovenia and Serbia. The pieces are suitable for intermediate and advanced players.

I would like to express my gratitude to Dr. James Sclater for his encouragement and brilliant musical suggestions, and to Dr. John Ingwerson for his proof reading and fingering ideas.

Tanja Mirić

Contents

Kraj tanana šadrvana

(At a Small Fountain)

Traditional Bosnian Song

arr. Tanja Mirić

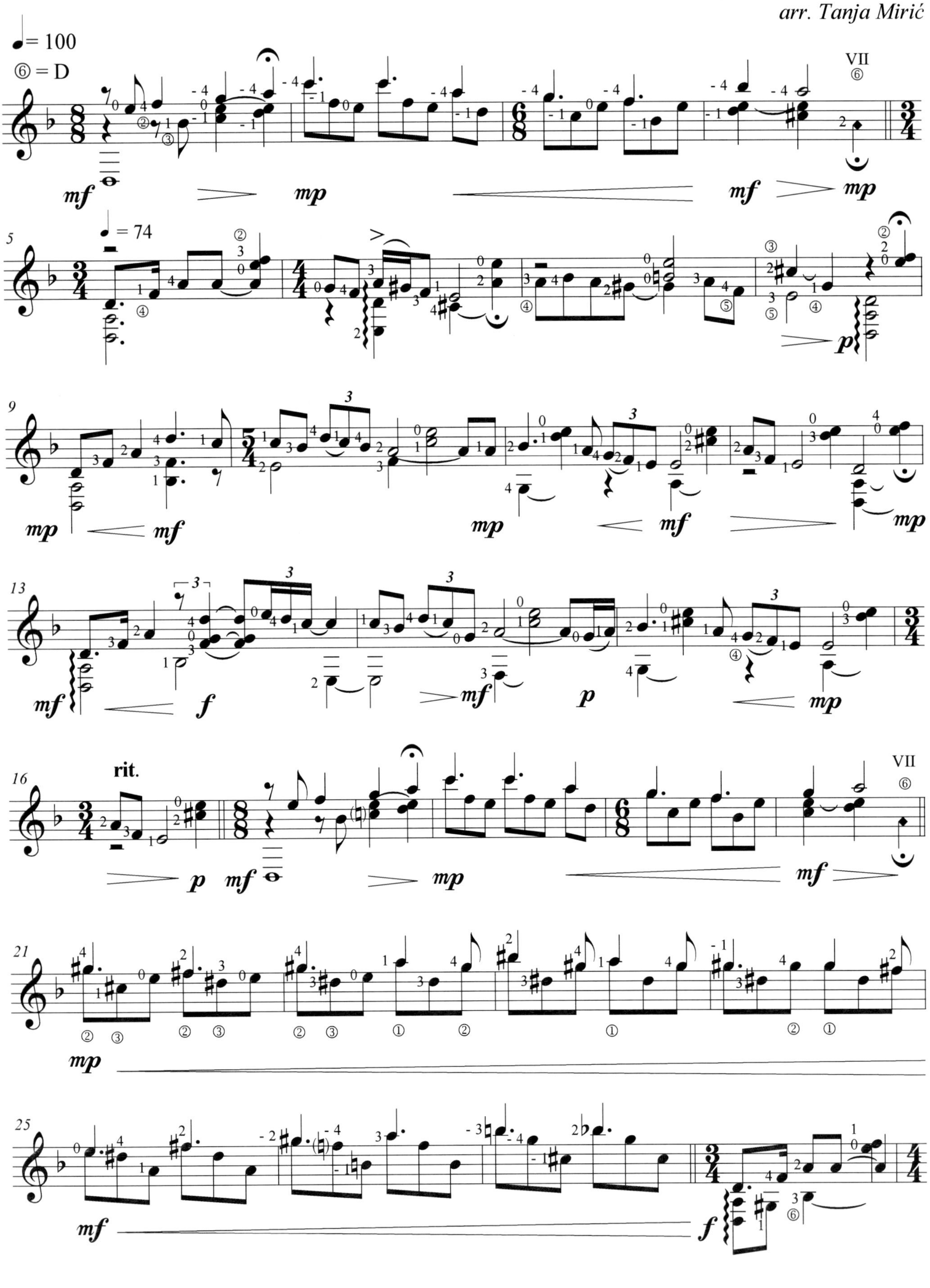

♩= 100

⑥ = D

♩ = 74

rit.

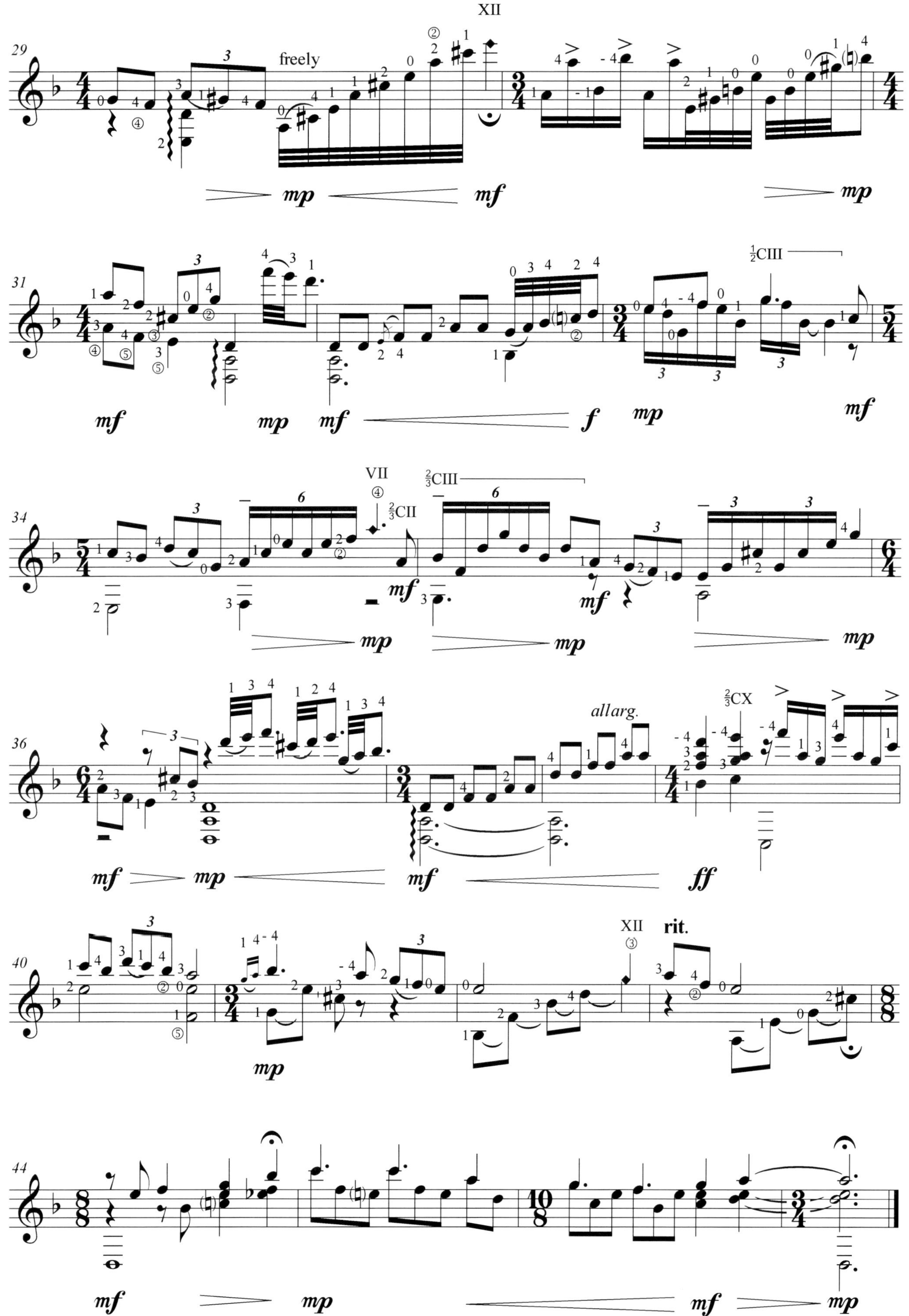
XII
freely
mp
mf
½CIII
f
VII
⅔CII
⅔CIII
allarg.
⅔CX
ff
rit.

Moj dilbere

(My Darling)

Traditional Bosnian Song

arr. Tanja Mirić

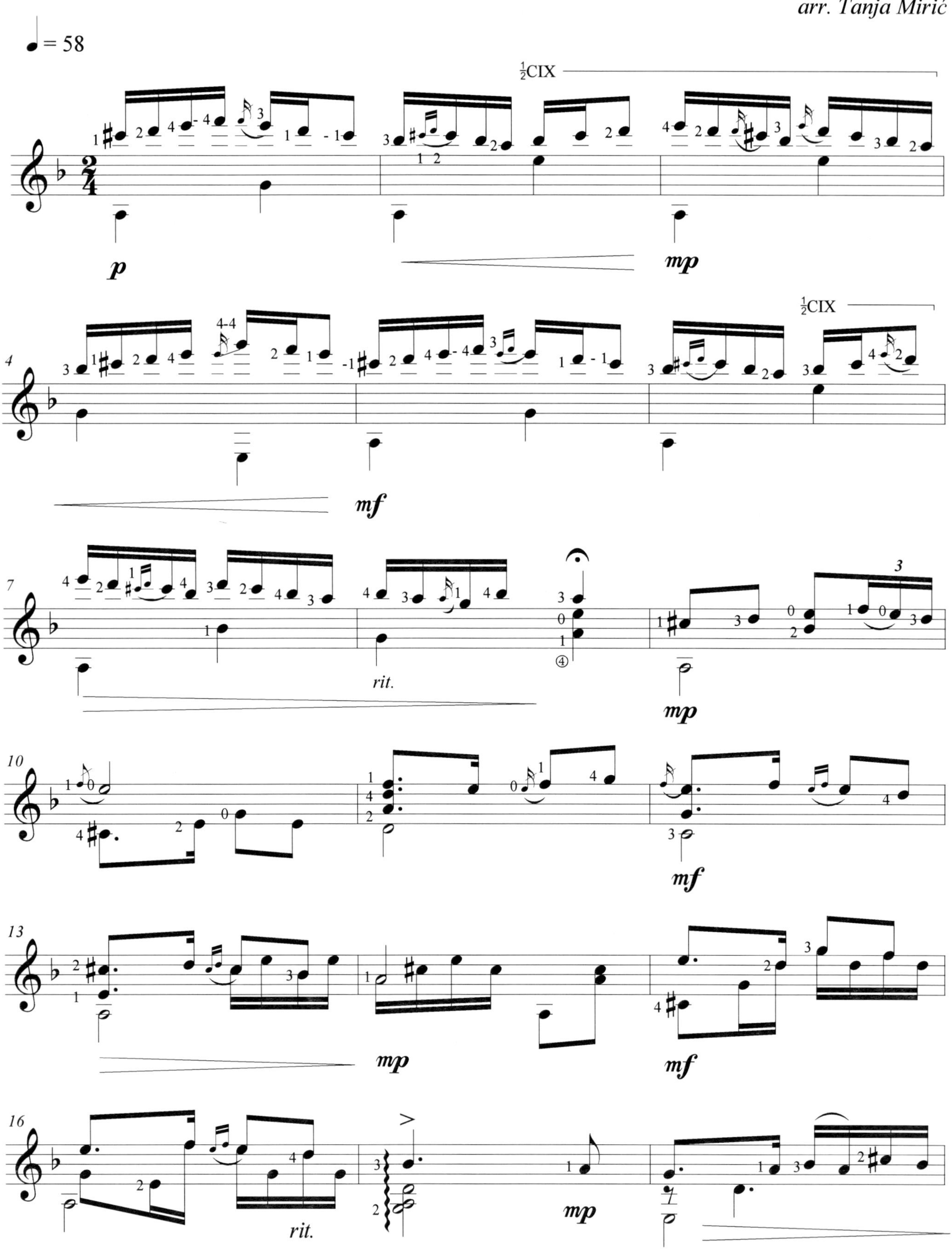

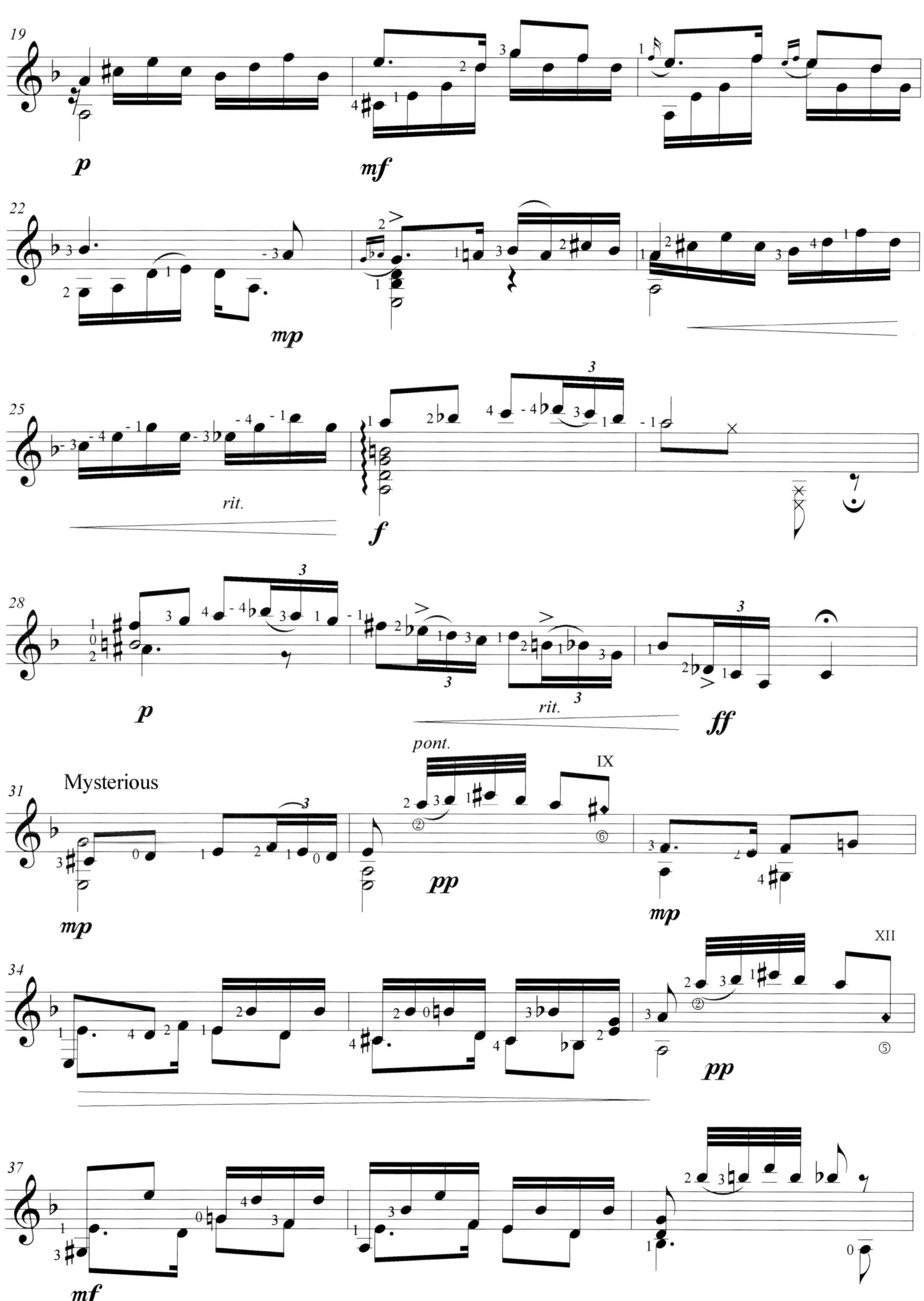
p
mf
mp
rit.
f
ff
Mysterious
pont.
IX
pp
XII

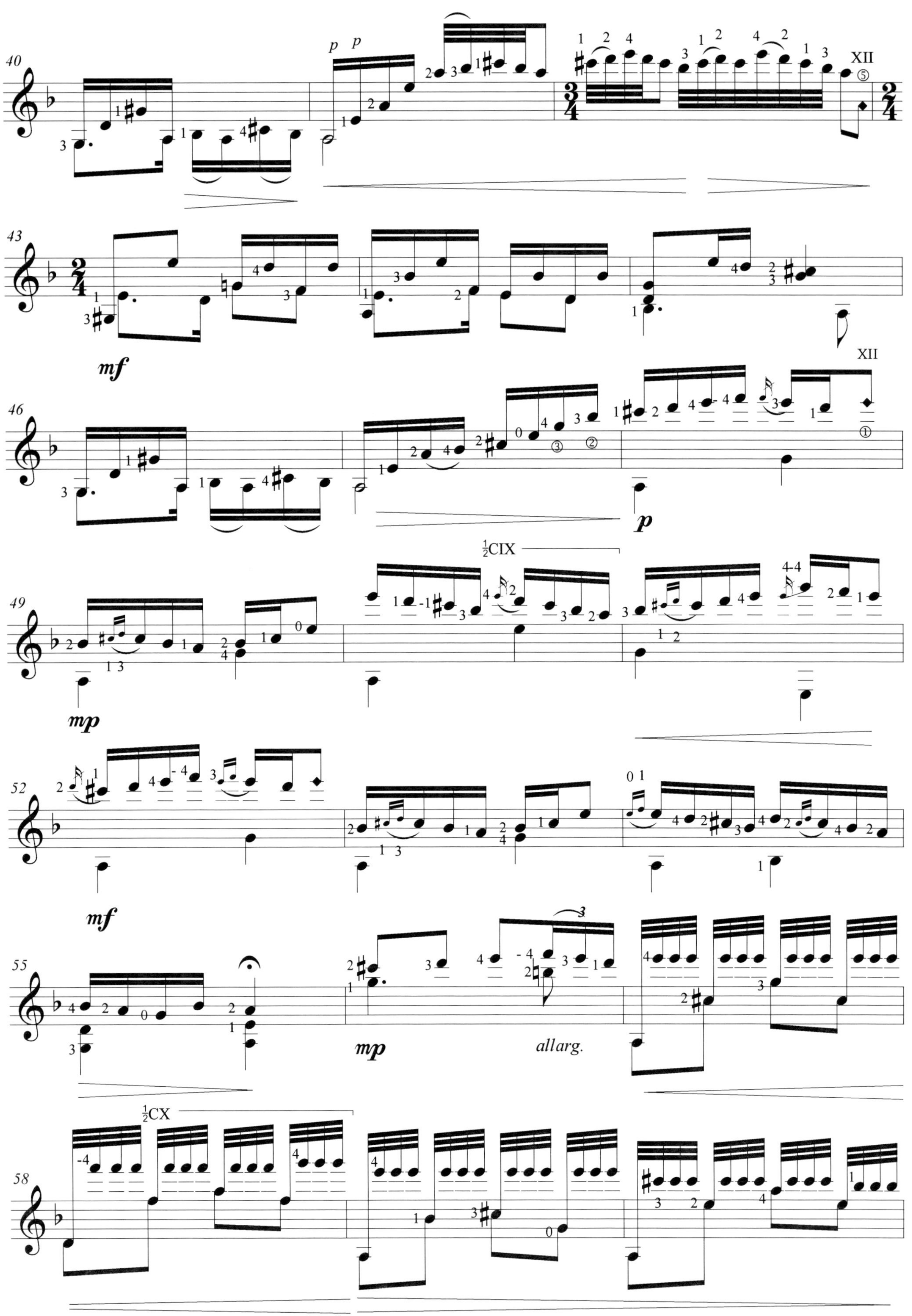

40
43
46
49
52
55
58
XII
½CIX
½CX
mf
p
mp
allarg.

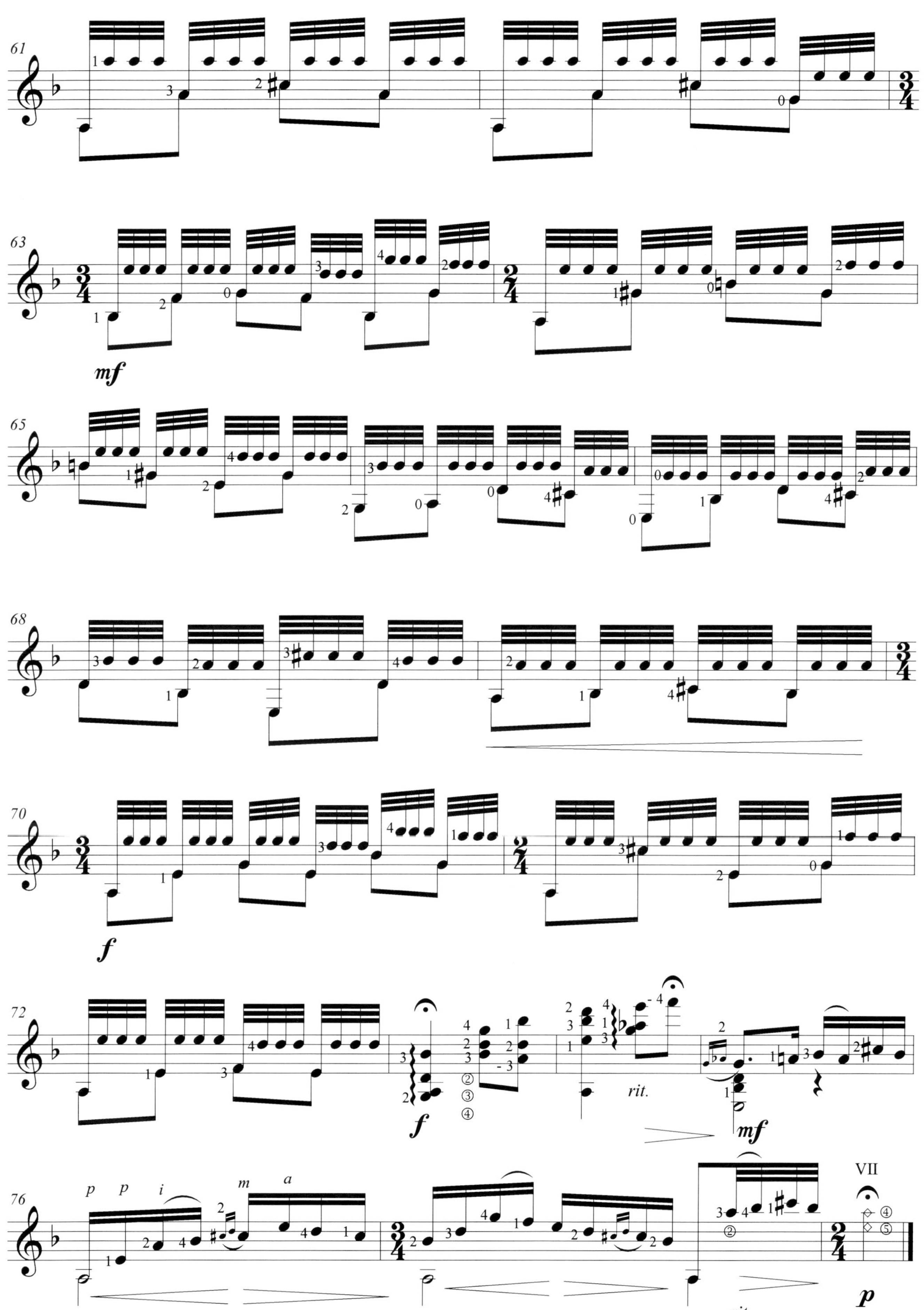

mf
f
rit.
mf
p p i m a
VII
rit..
p

More sokol pie

(Behold, a Falcon is Drinking)

Traditional Macedonian Song

arr. Tanja Mirić

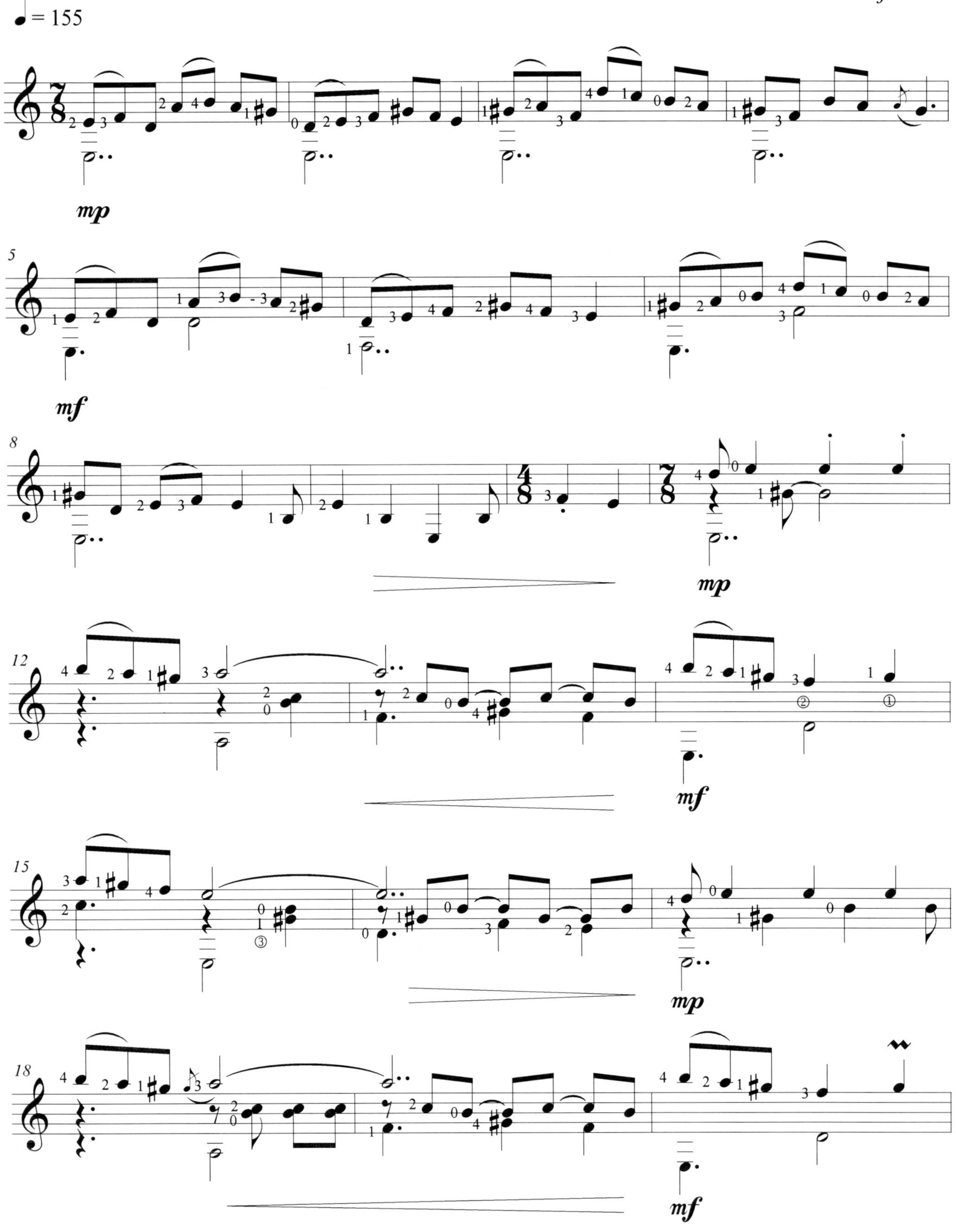

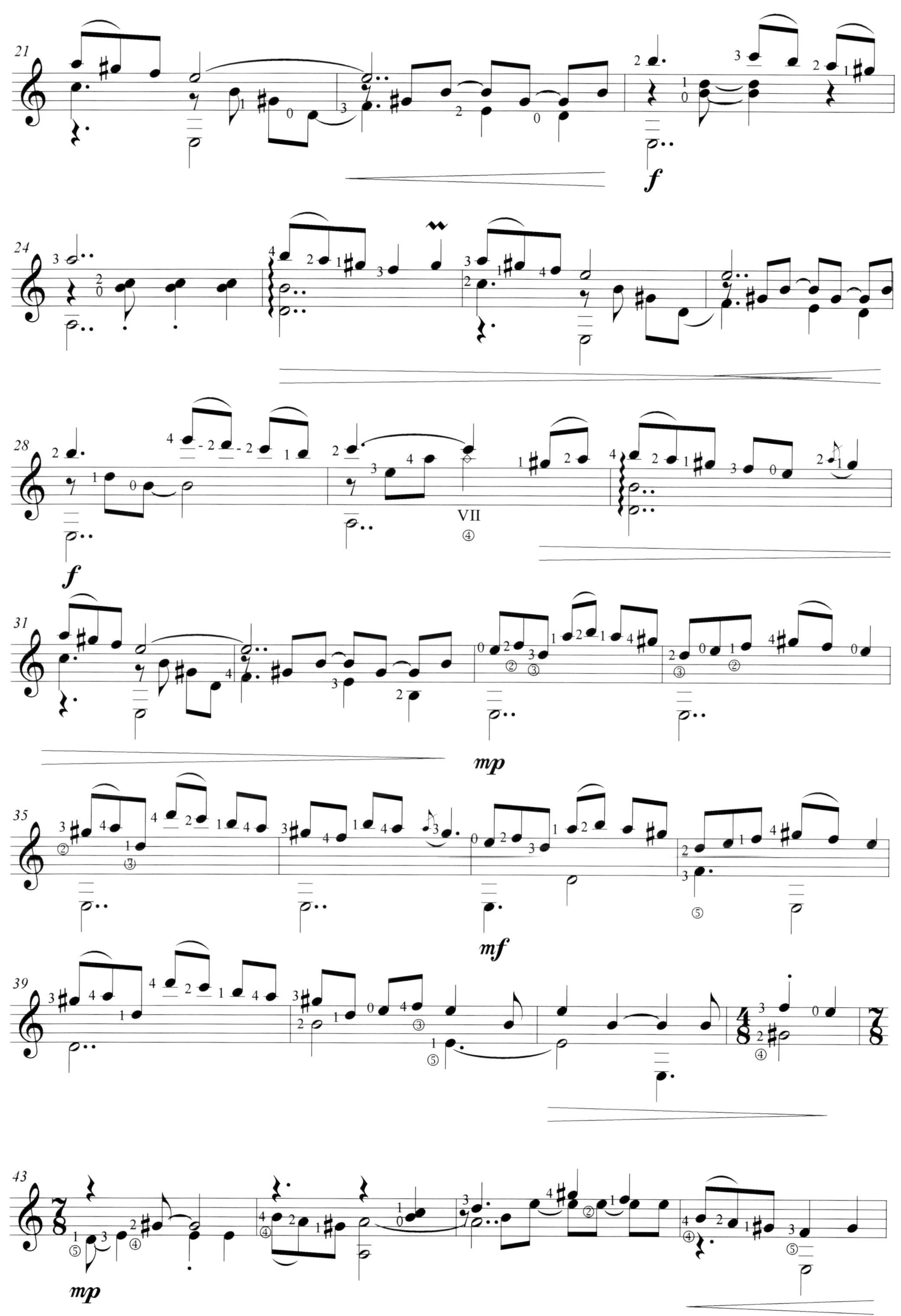
f
f
VII
mp
mf
mp

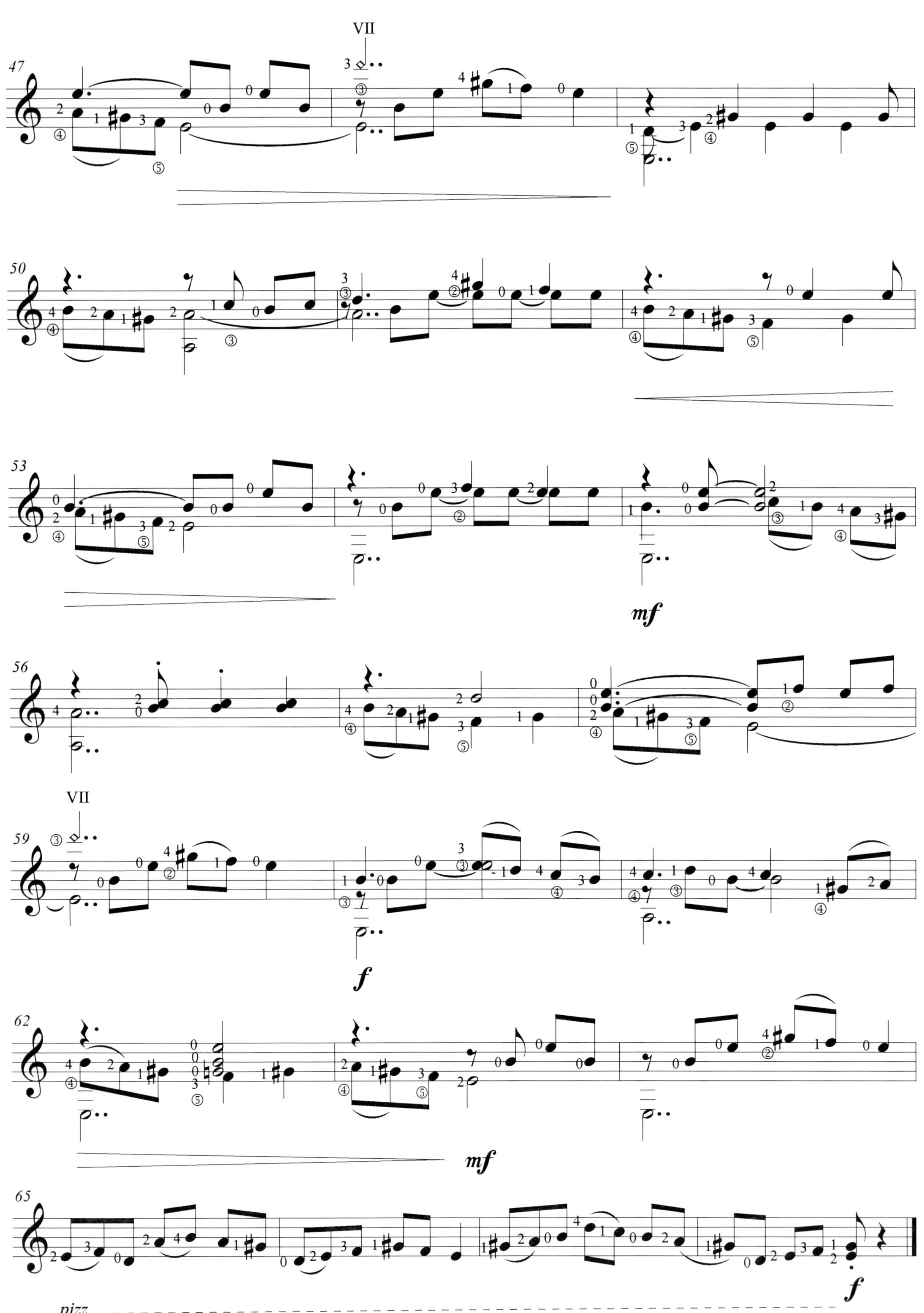
VII
mf
VII
f
mf
pizz.
f

Bun ii vinul ghiurghiuliu

(Good Rosy Wine)

Traditional Romanian Song
arr. Tanja Mirić

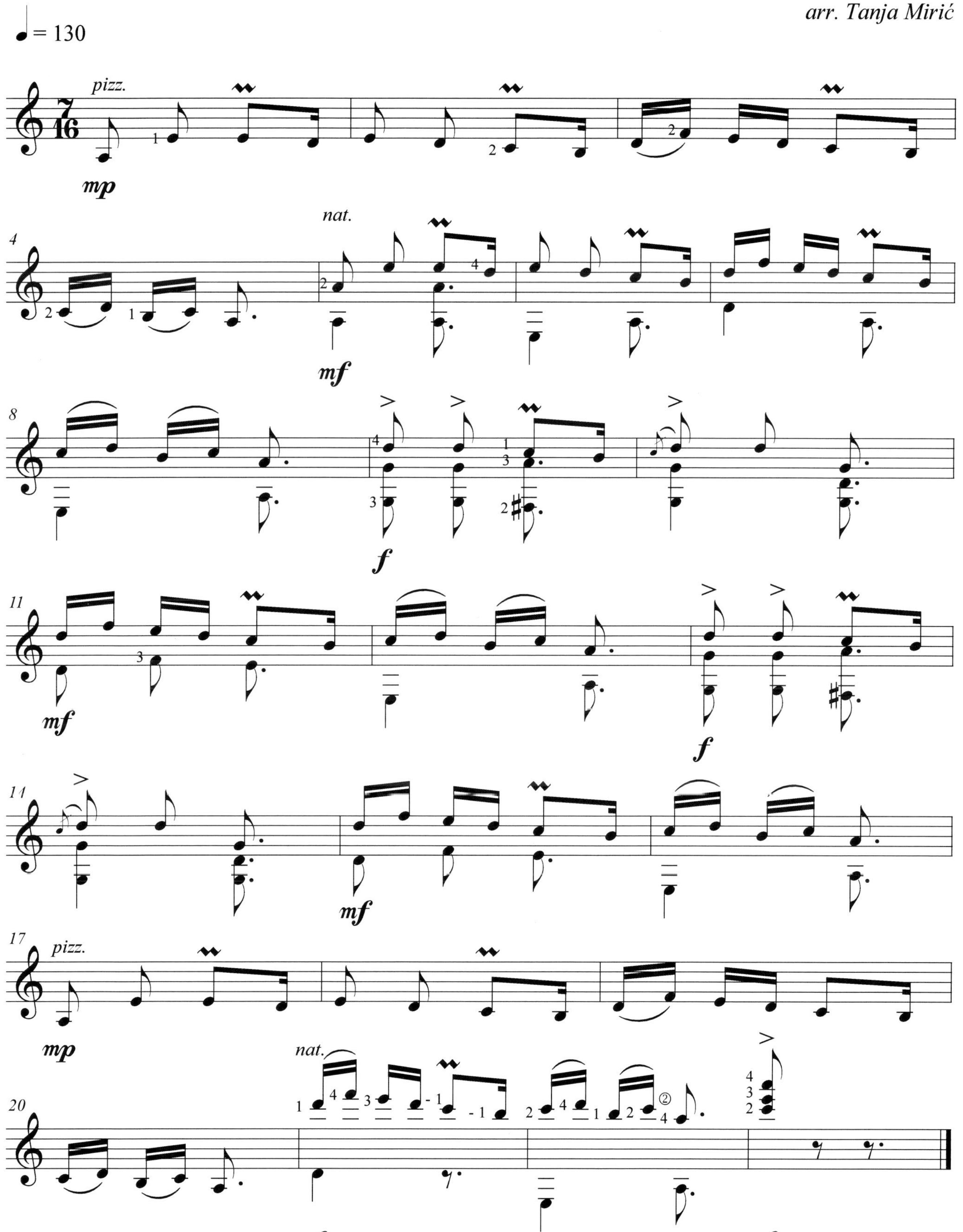

♩ = 130

pizz.

mp

4 *nat.*

mf

8

f

11

mf

f

14

mf

17 *pizz.*

mp

20 *nat.*

mf *f*

Brâu de la Făgăraş

(A Sash from Făgăraş)

Traditional Romanian Dance
arr. Tanja Mirić

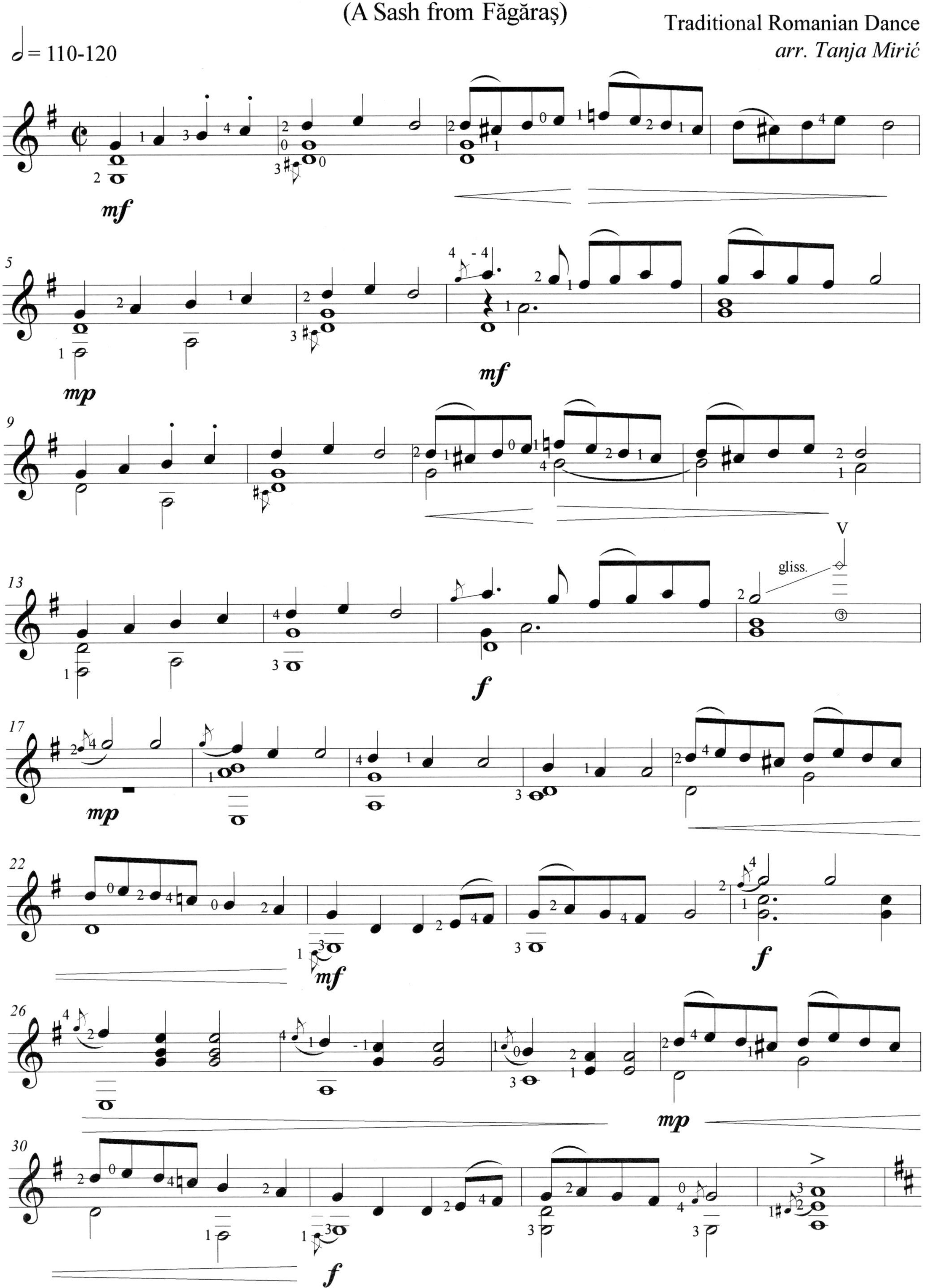

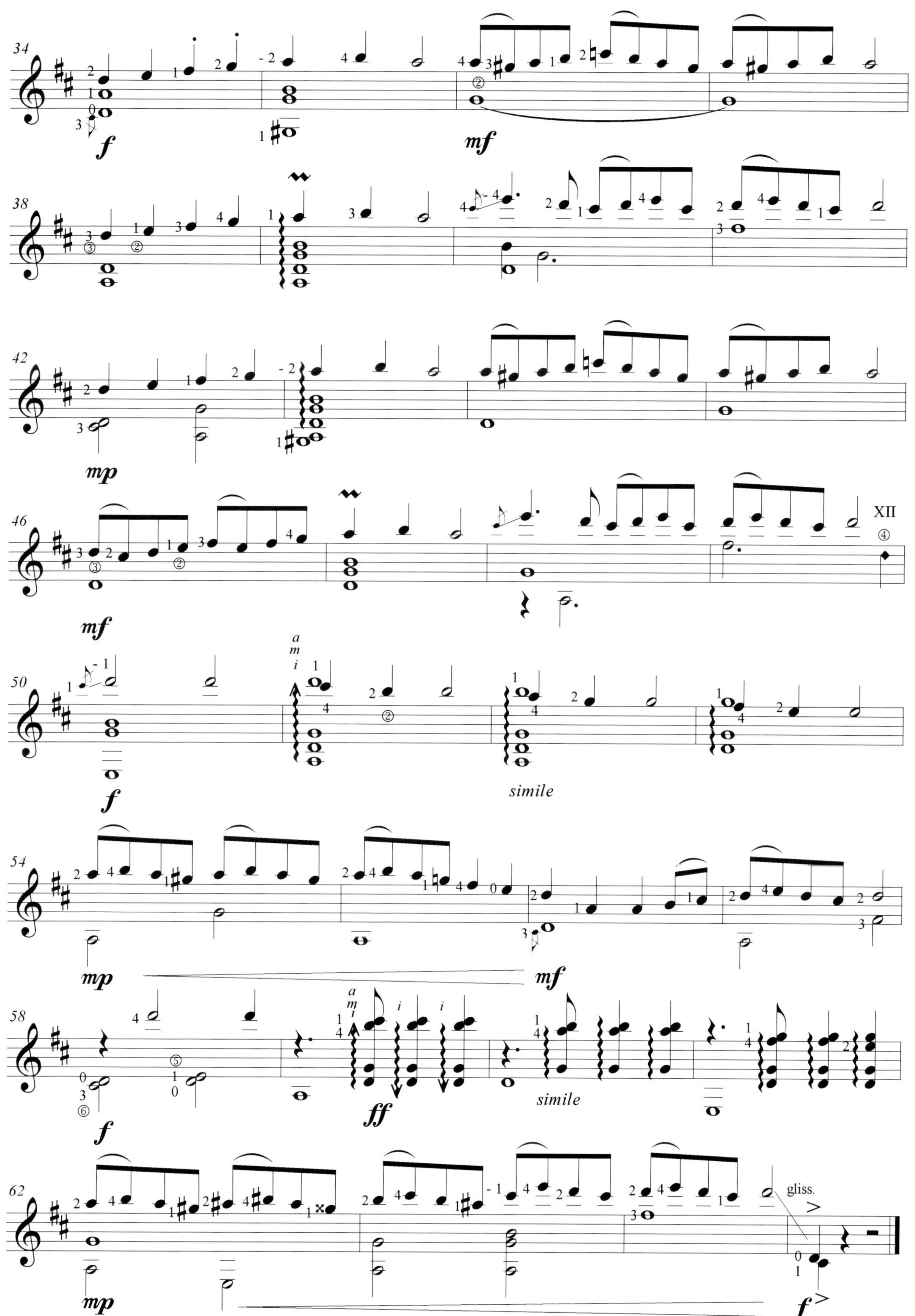
f
mf
mp
mf
XII
f
simile
mp
mf
f
ff
simile
mp
gliss.
f

Kara Üzüm

(Dark Blue Grapes)

Traditional Turkish Melody

arr. Tanja Mirić

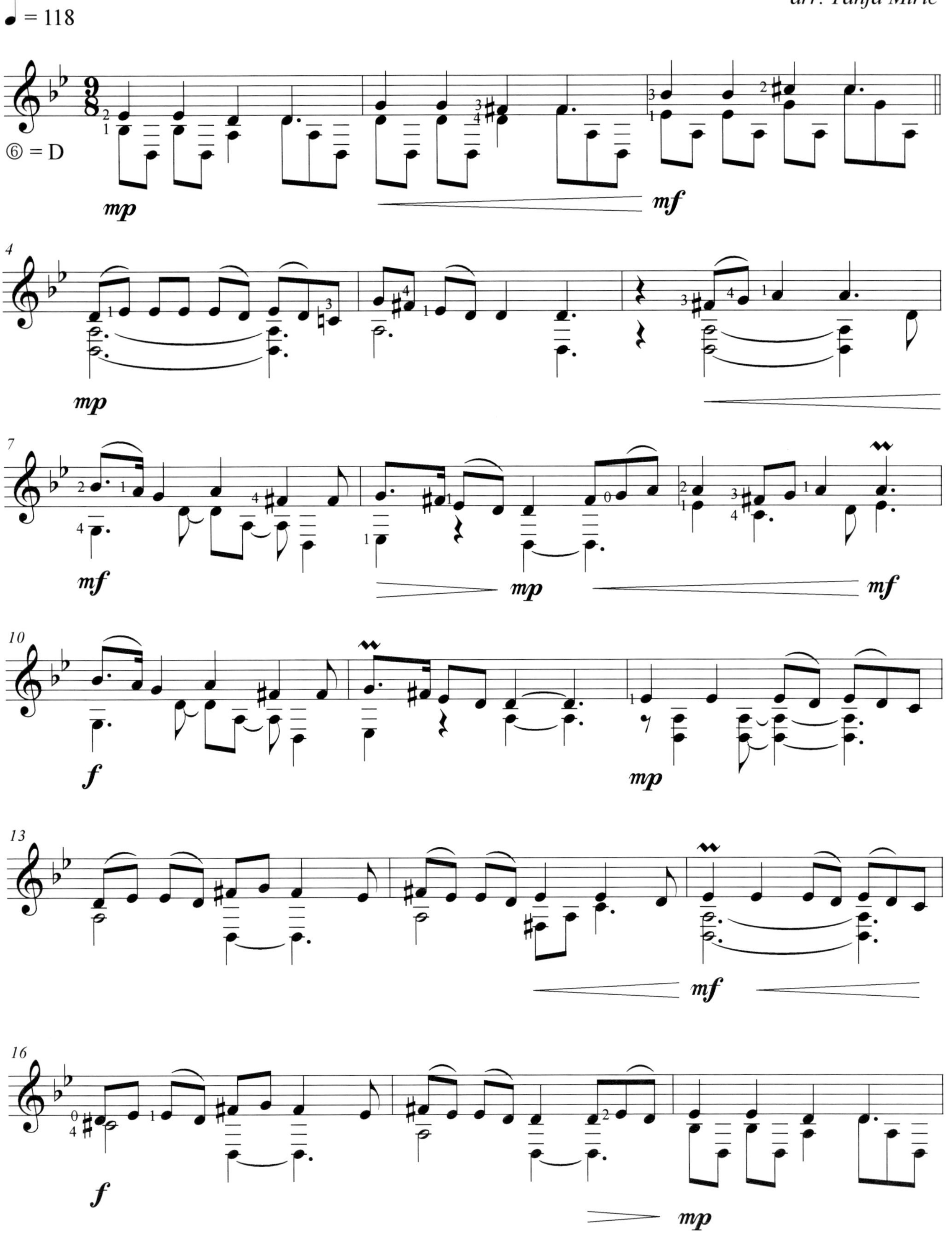

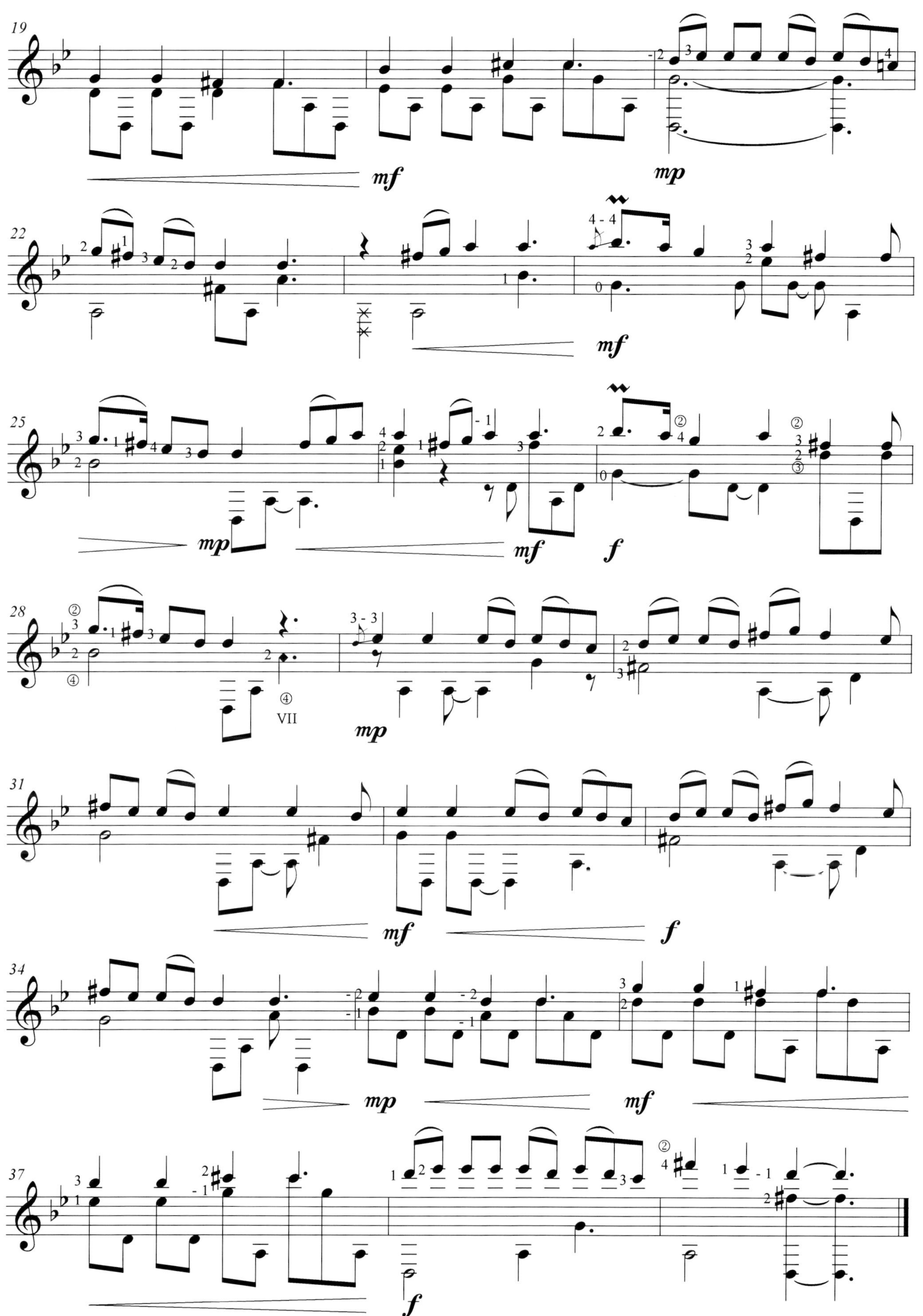
19
mf
mp
22
mf
25
mp
mf
f
28
VII
mp
31
mf
f
34
mp
mf
37
f

Oğlum Oğlum

(My Boy, My Boy)

Traditional Turkish Song
arr. Tanja Mirić

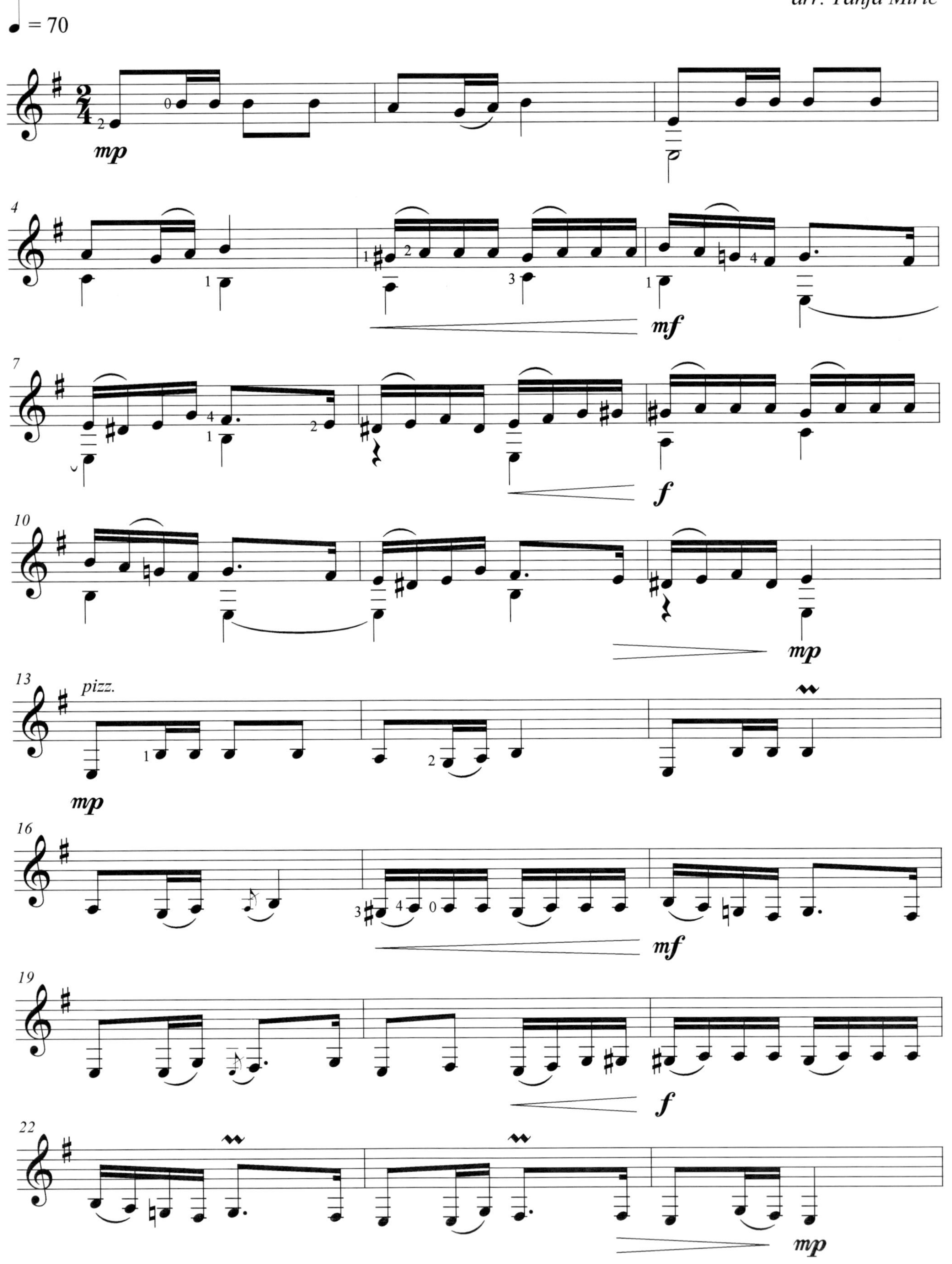

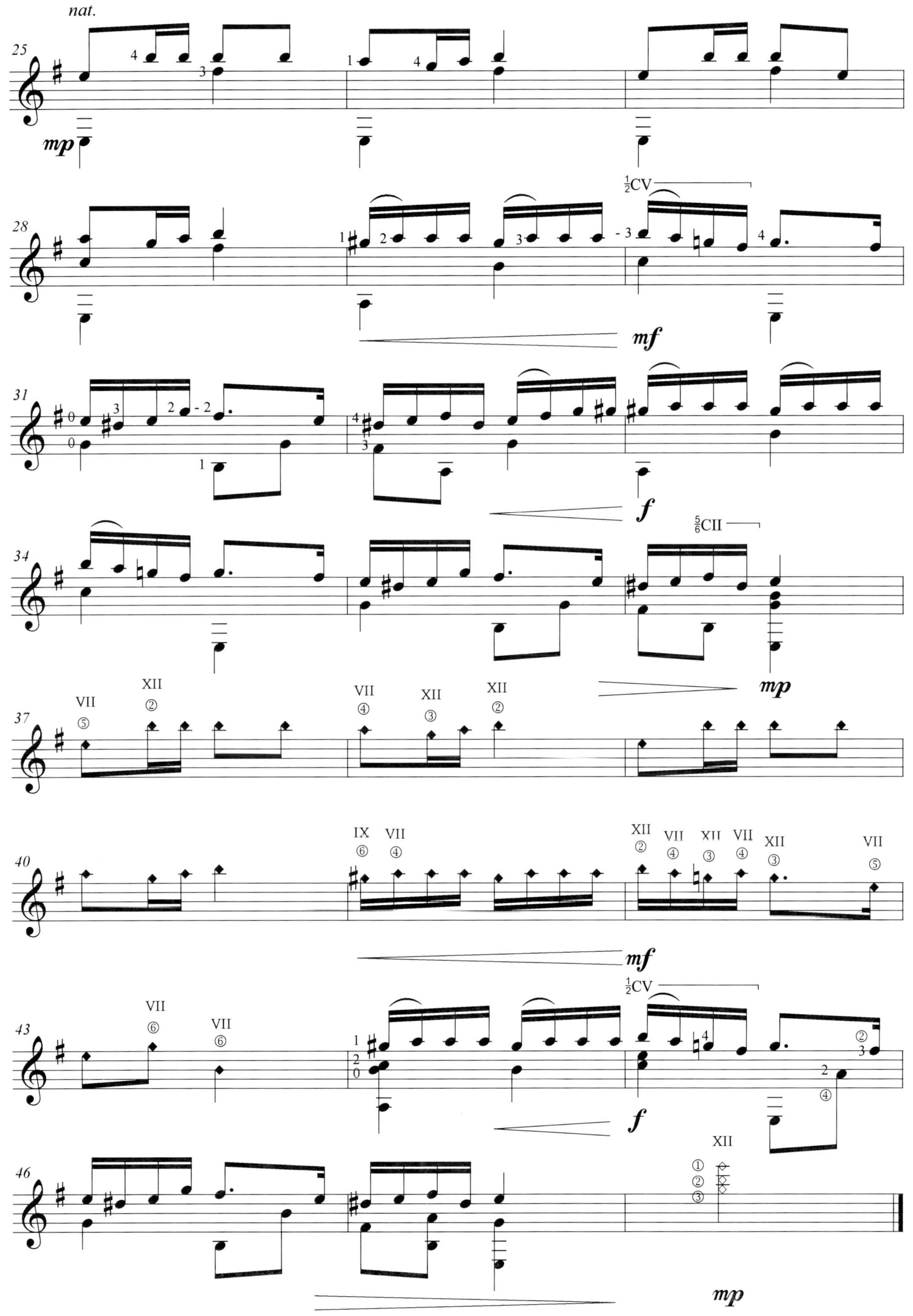
nat.
mp
½CV
mf
f
⅚CII
mp
VII
XII
IX
mf
½CV
f
XII
mp

Yerakina

Traditional Greek Song
arr. Tanja Mirić

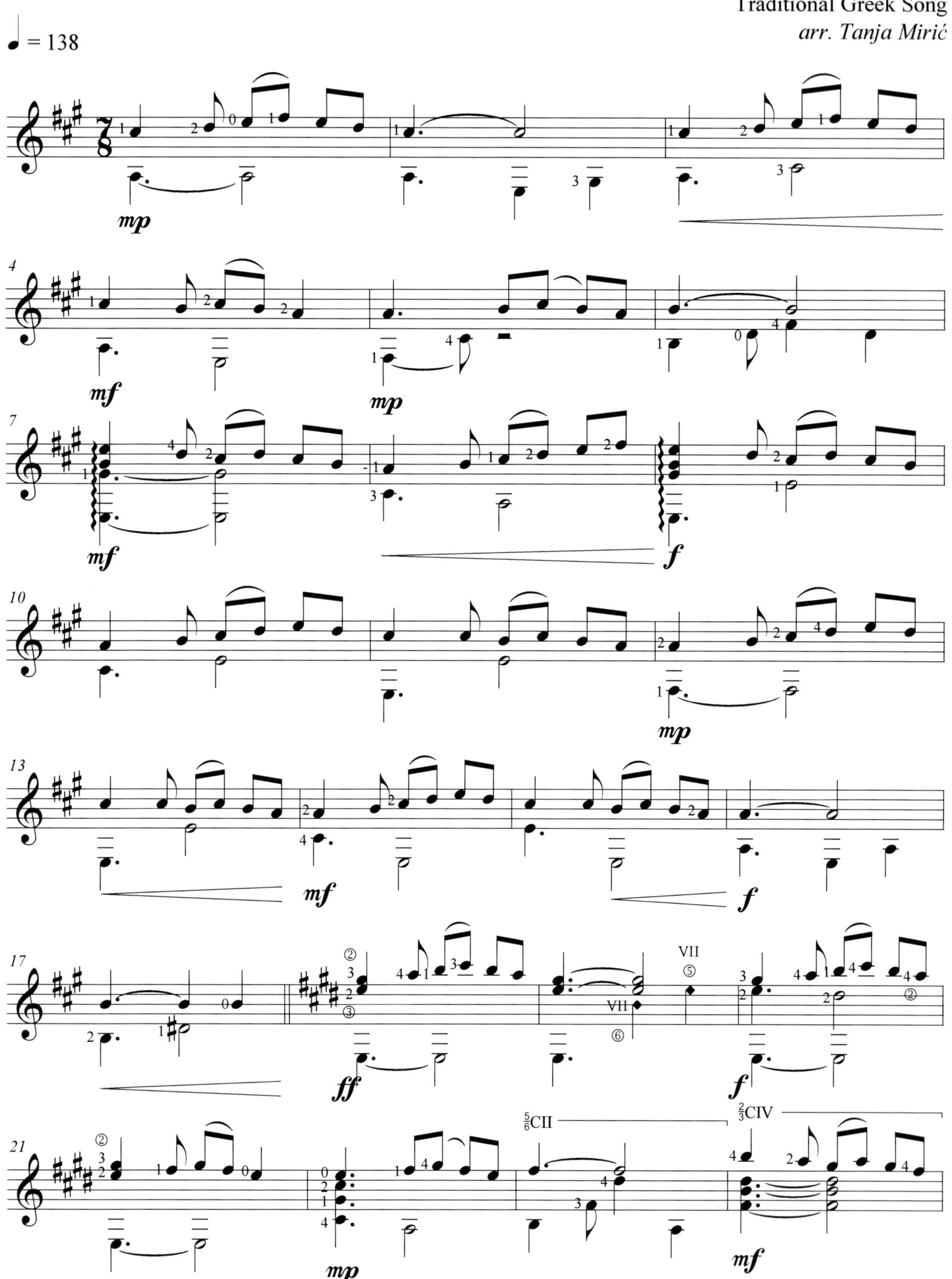

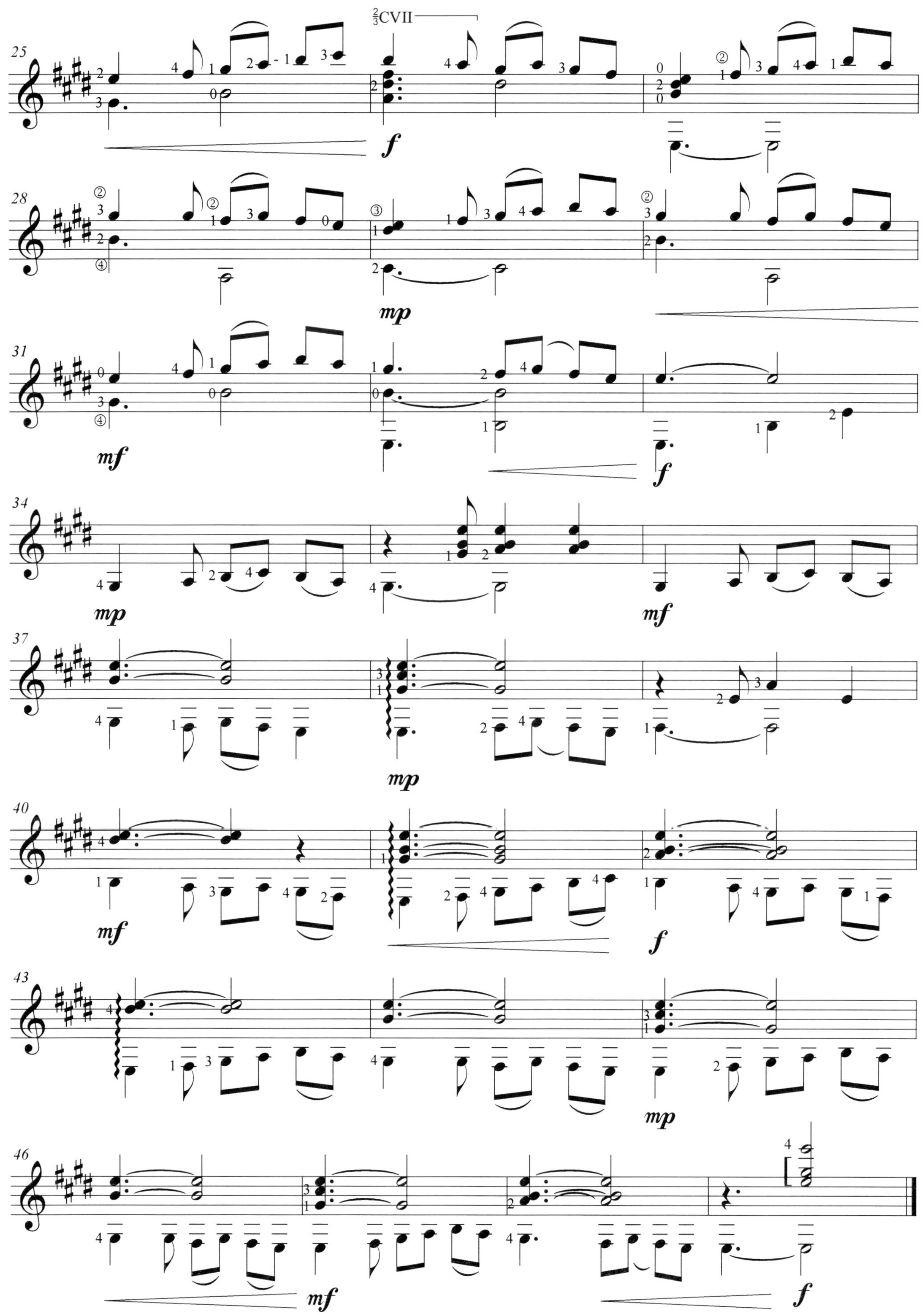

⅔CVII

Misirlou

(Egyptian)

Traditional Greek Song

arr. Tanja Mirić

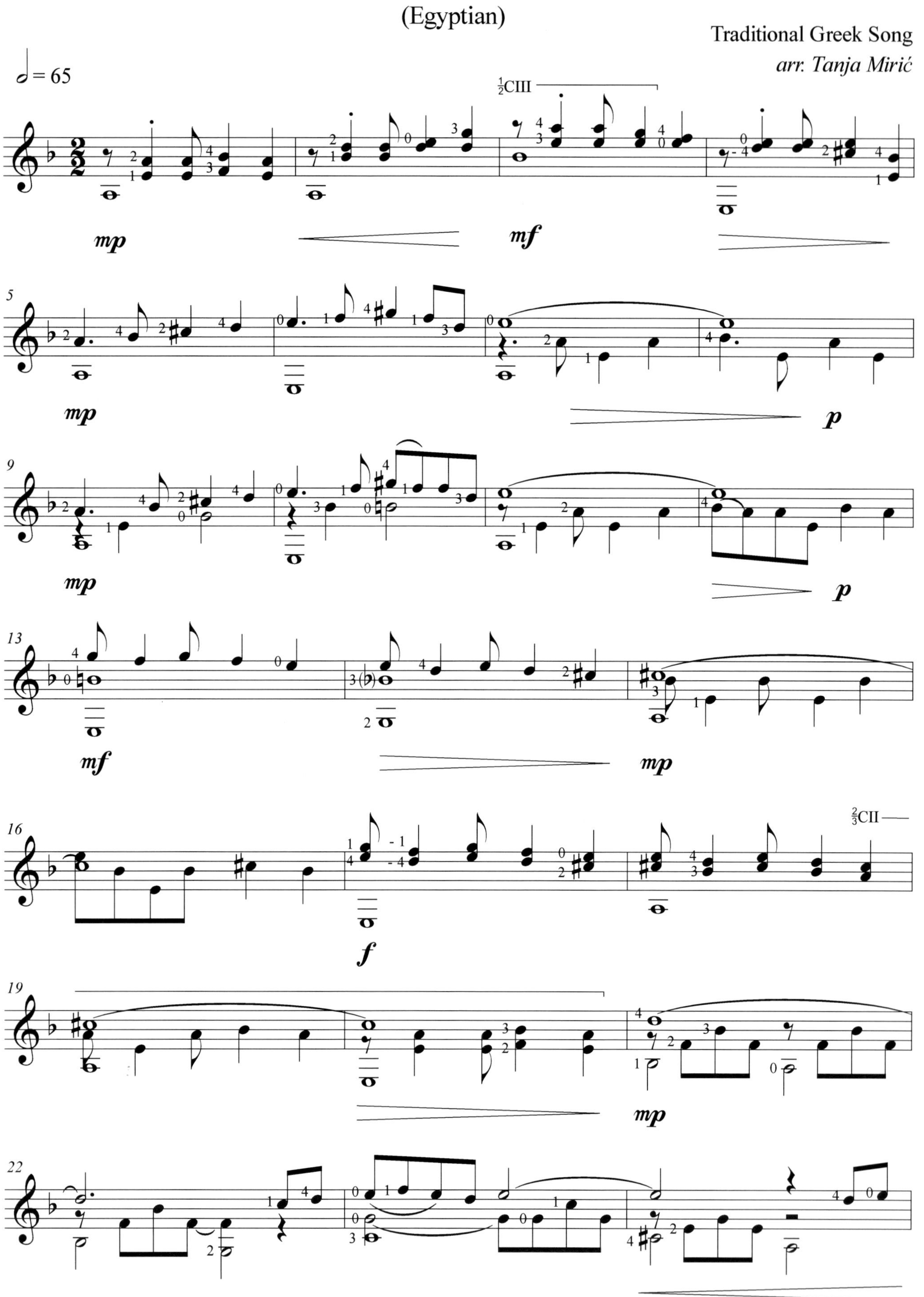

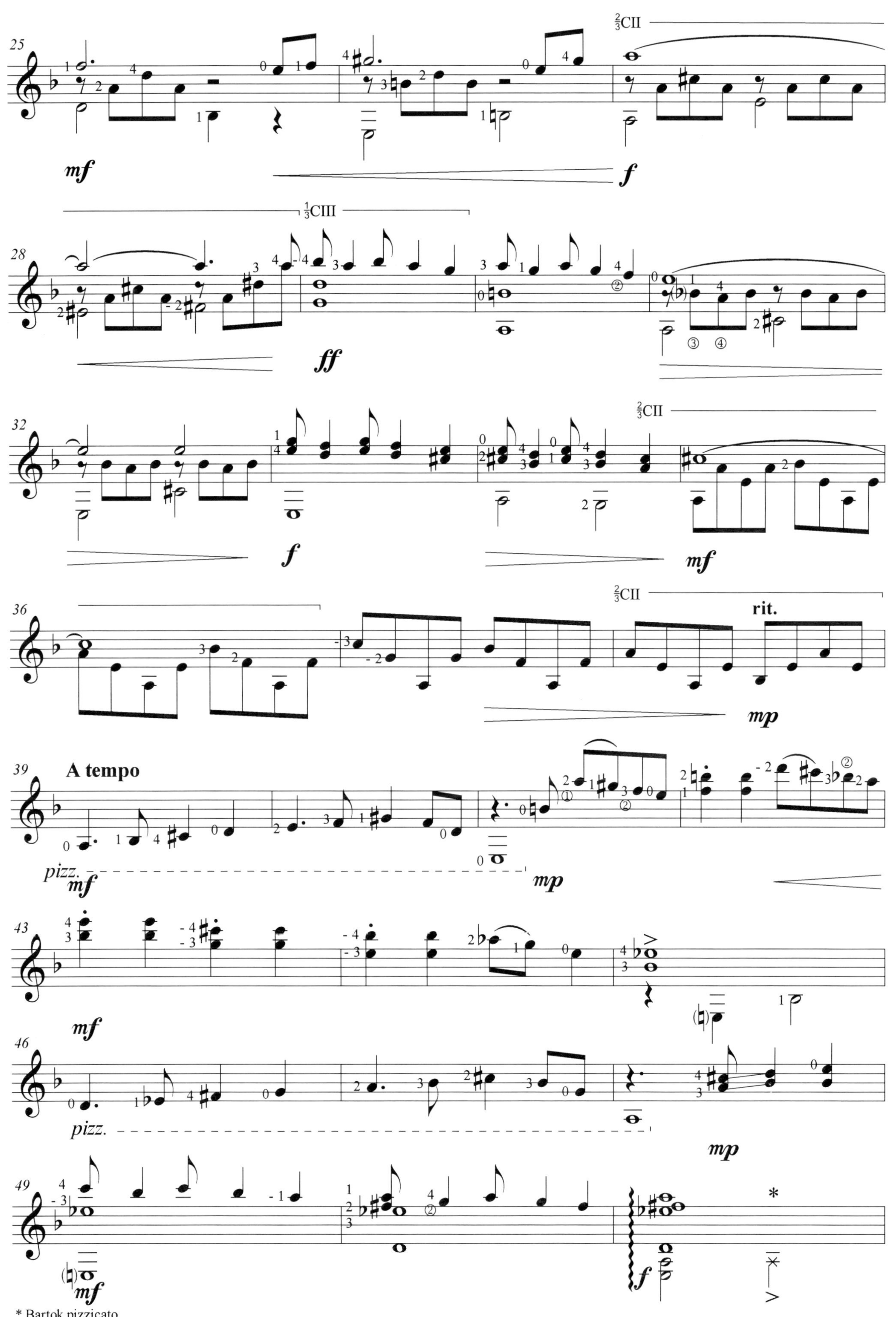
mf
f
ff
rit.
mp
A tempo
pizz.
* Bartok pizzicato

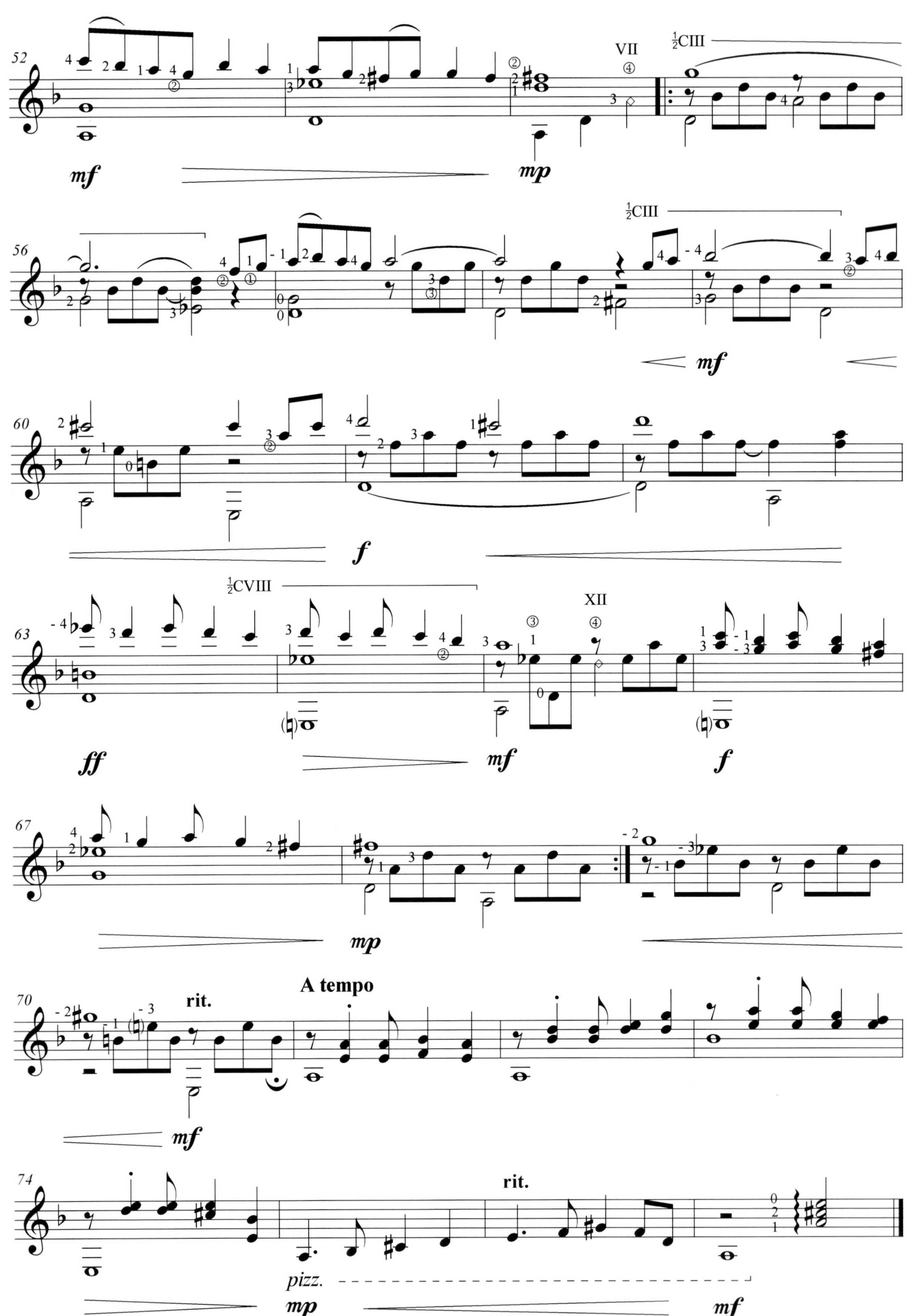
VII
½CIII
½CIII
½CVIII
XII
rit.
A tempo
rit.
pizz.

Dunave, tiha vodo hladna

(The Quiet Cold Waters of the Danube)

Traditional Serbian Song
arr. Tanja Mirić

Allegro

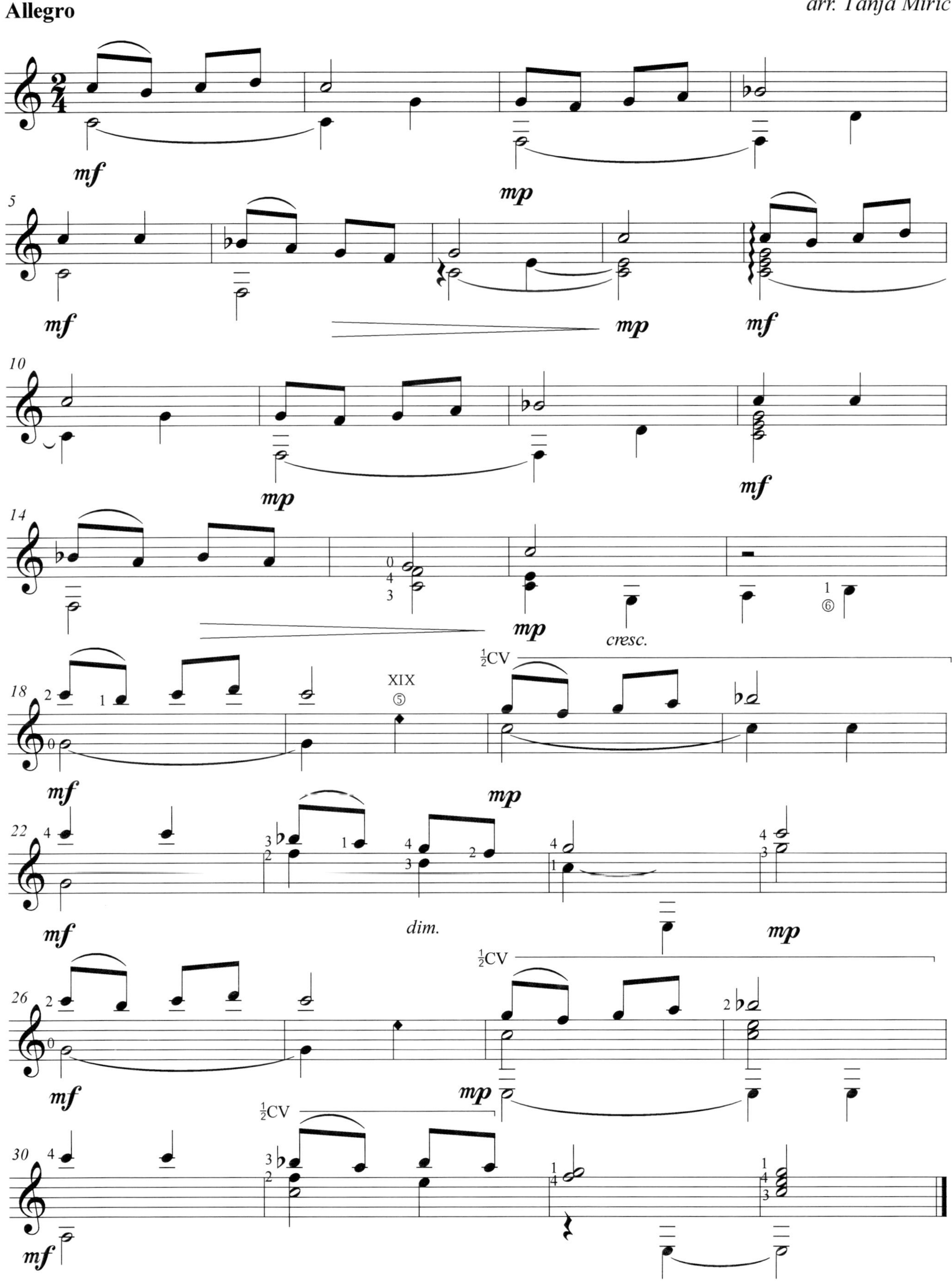

Užičko kolo

(Dance from Užice)

Traditional Serbian Dance
arr. Tanja Mirić

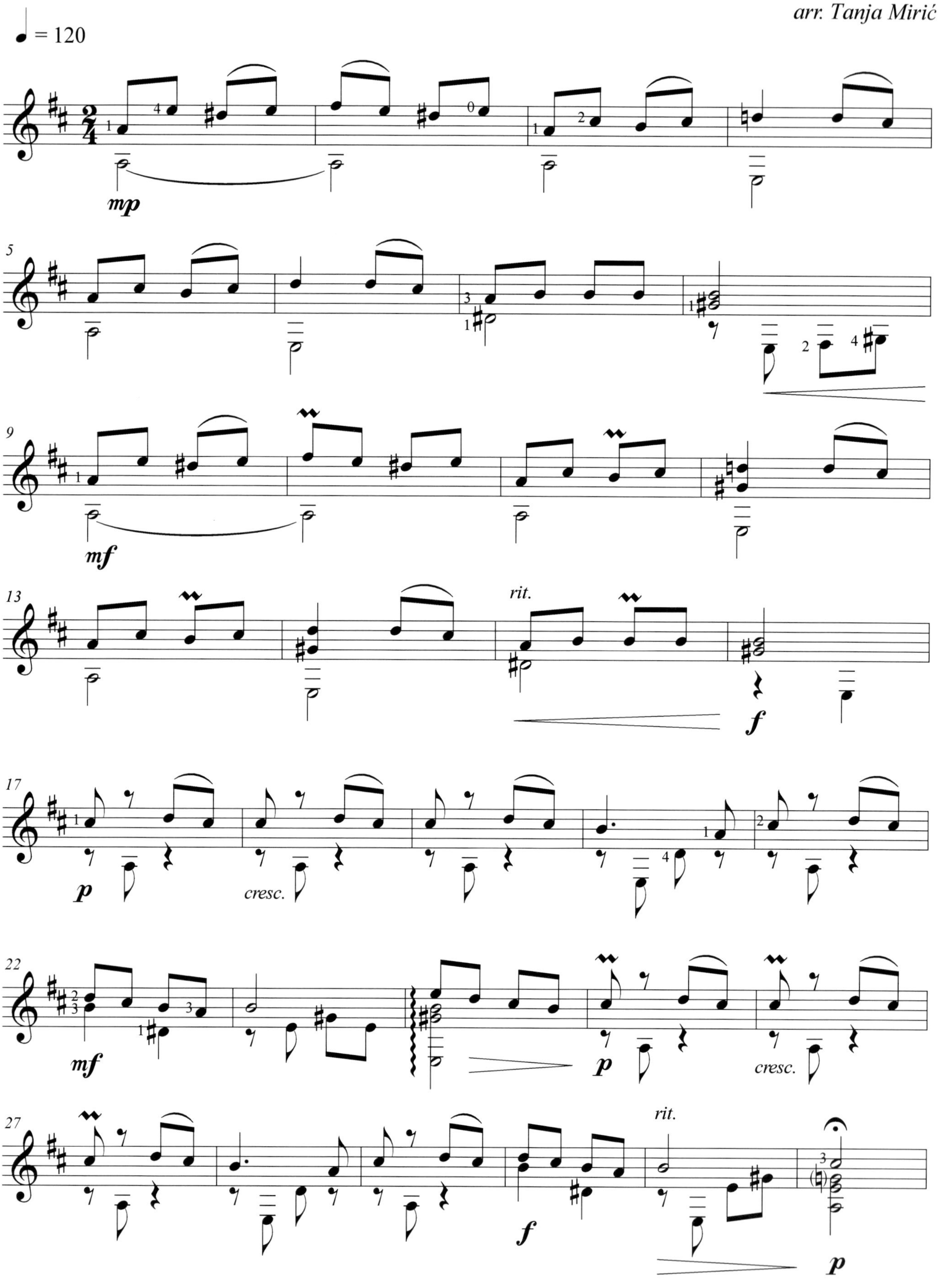

♩ = 120

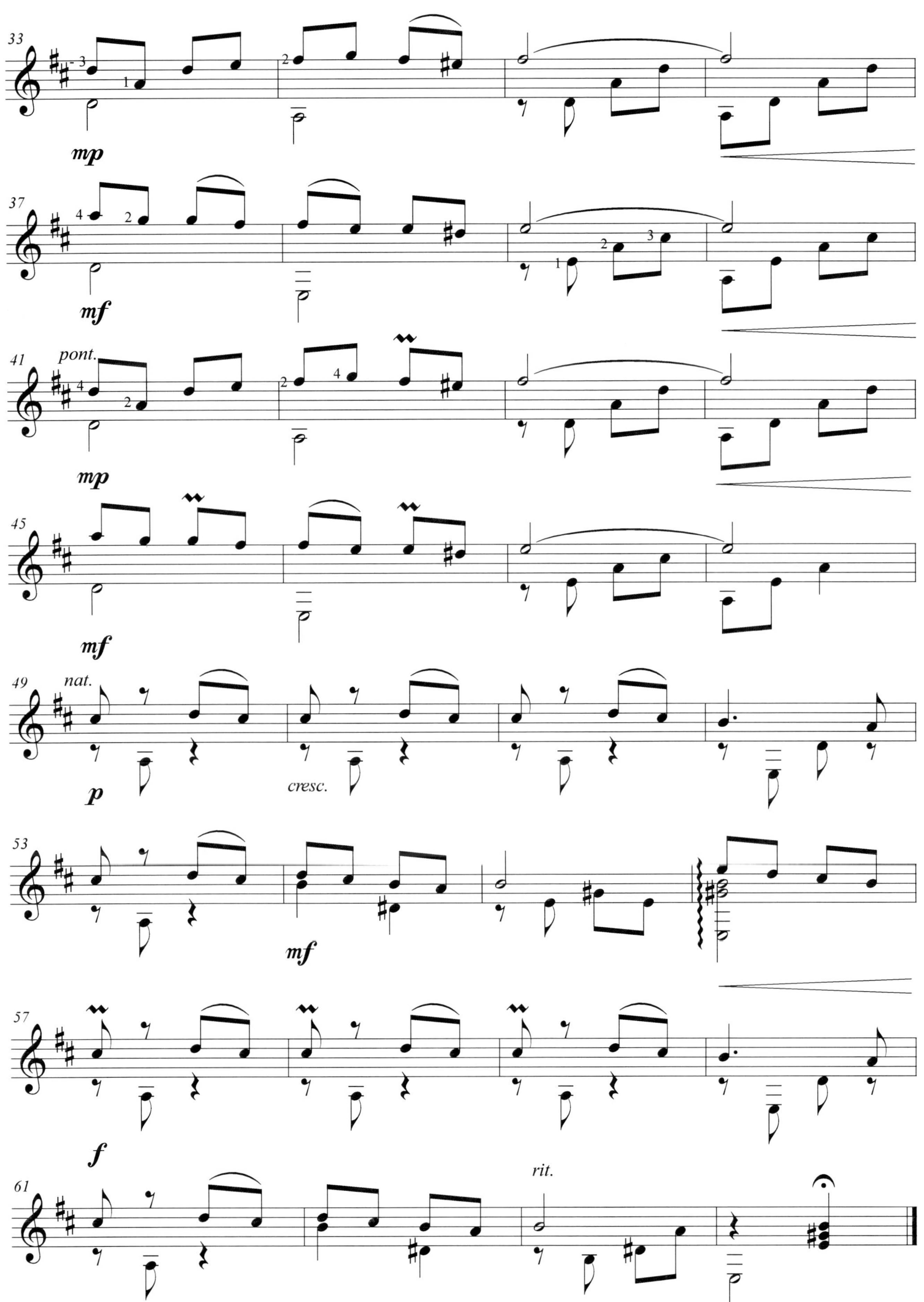
33
mp
37
mf
41
pont.
mp
45
mf
49
nat.
p
cresc.
53
mf
57
f
61
rit.

Jaz pa pojdem na Gorenjsko

(I am Going to Gorenjska)

Traditional Slovenian Song

arr. Tanja Mirić

Allegro

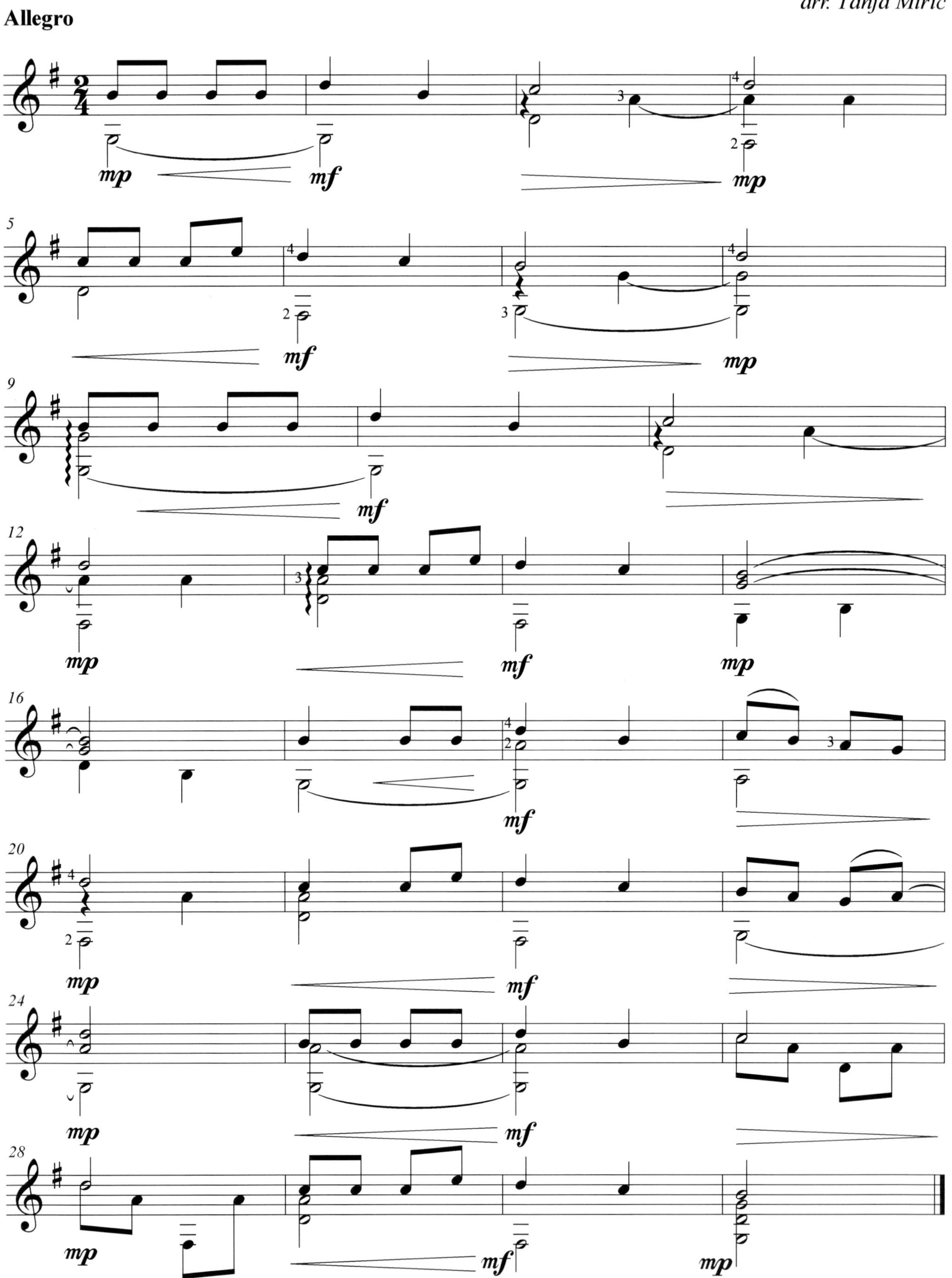

Moj očka ma konjička dva

(My Father Has Two Ponies)

Traditional Slovenian Song
arr. Tanja Mirić

Allegro

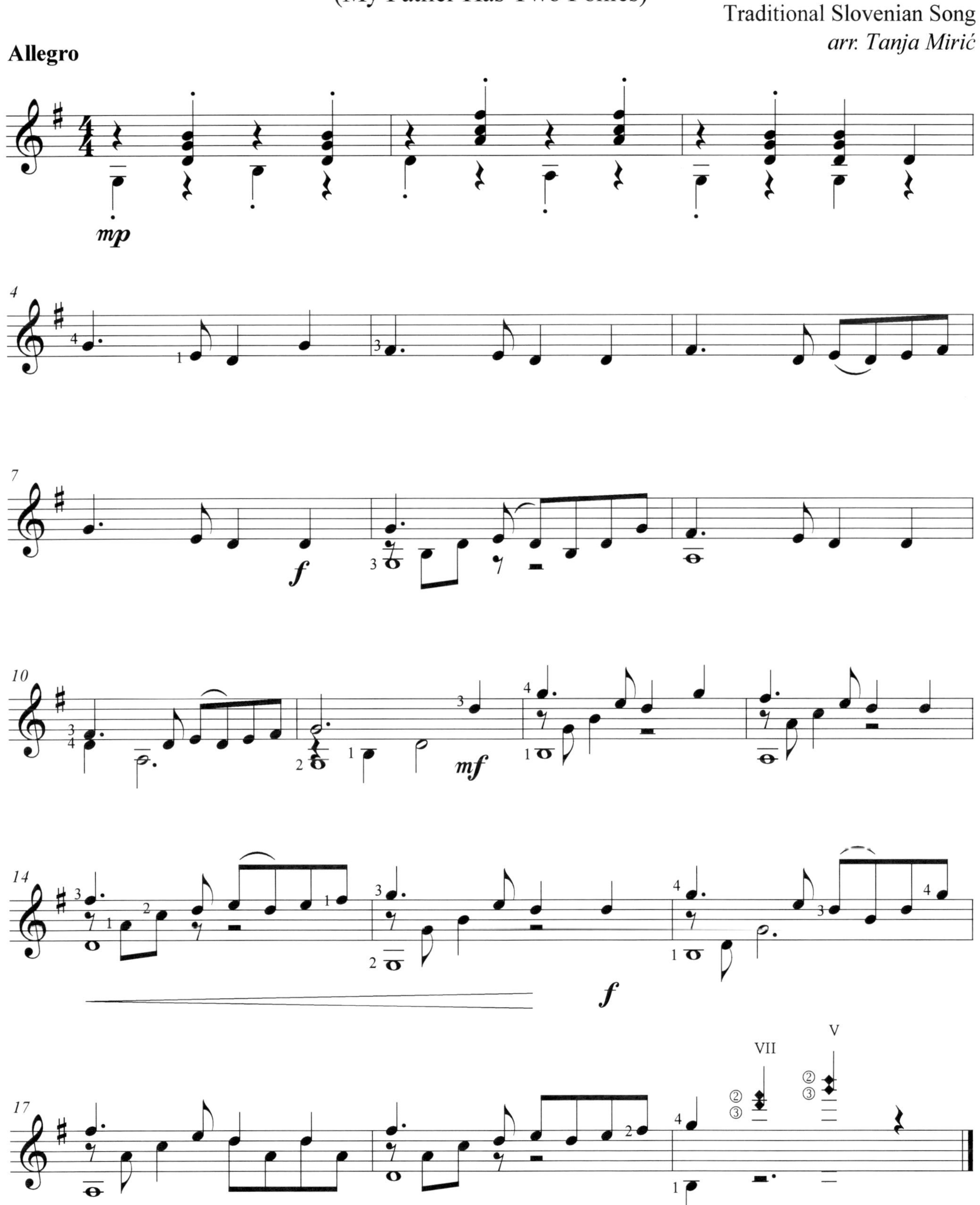

Sve ptičice iz gore

(All the Birds from the Hill)

Traditional Croatian Song
arr. Tanja Mirić

Allegretto

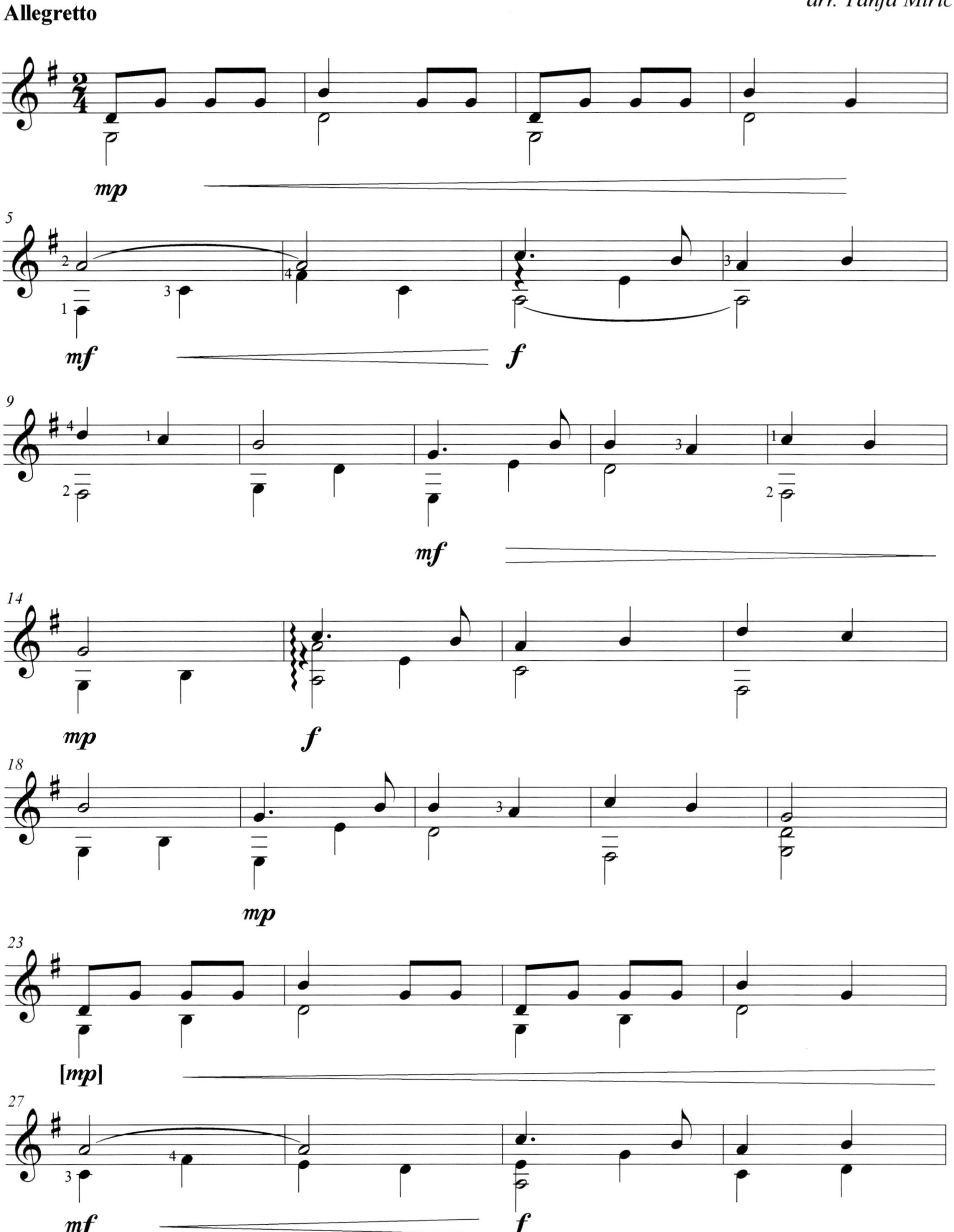

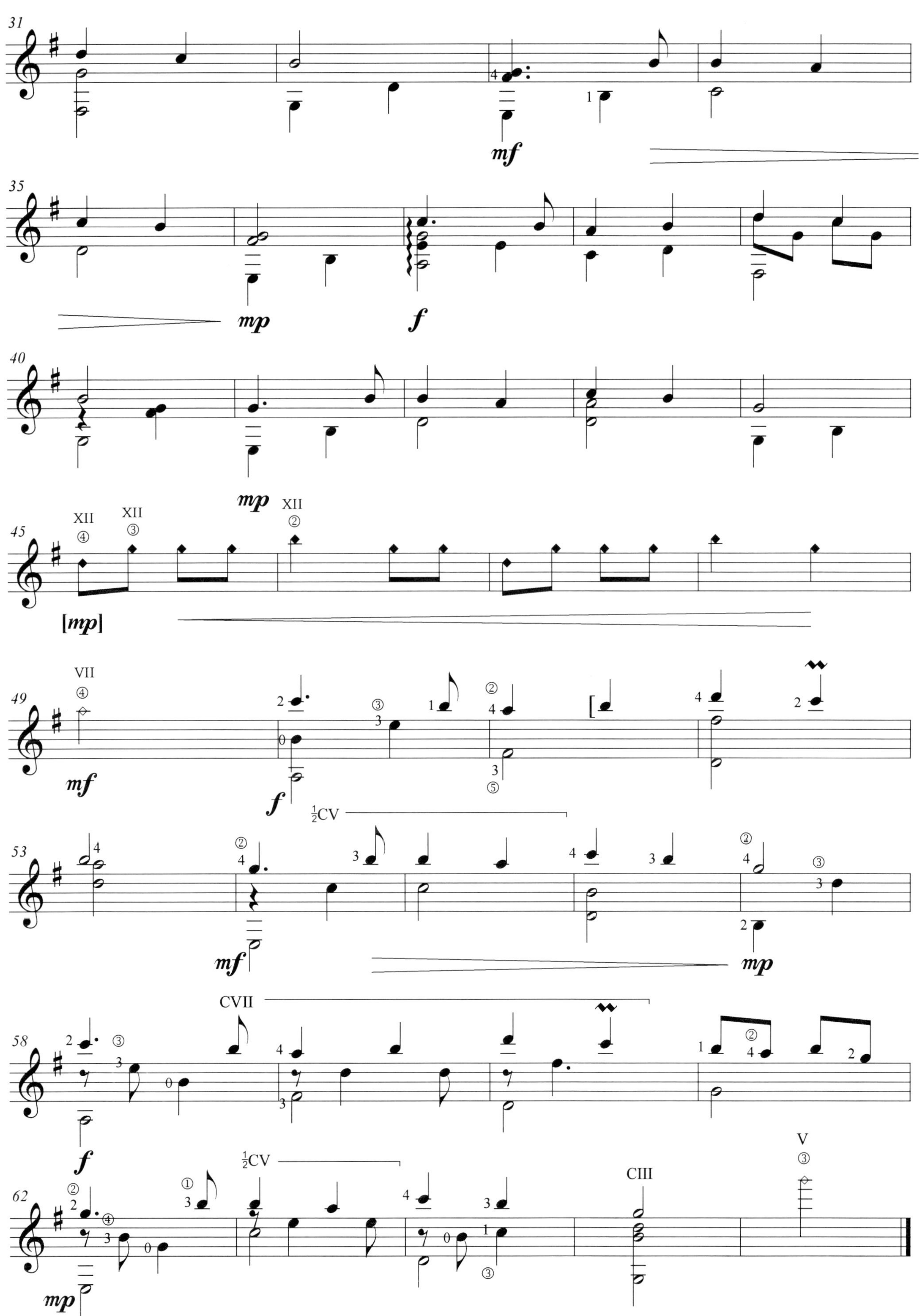
mf
mp
f
[mp]
XII
VII
1/2CV
CVII
CIII
V

Ta divna splitska noć

(Oh, What a Delightful Evening in Split)

Traditional Dalmatian Song
arr. Tanja Mirić

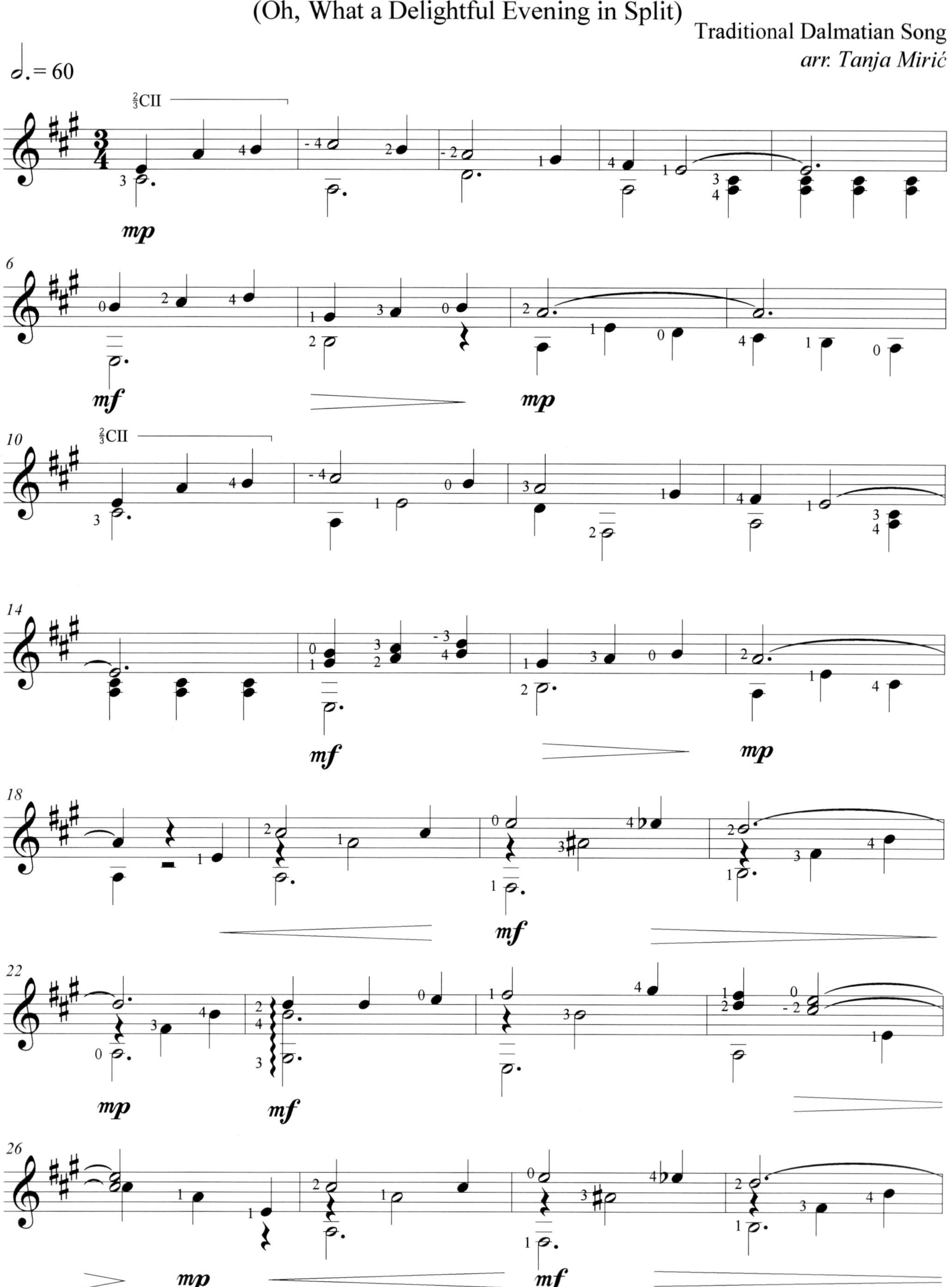

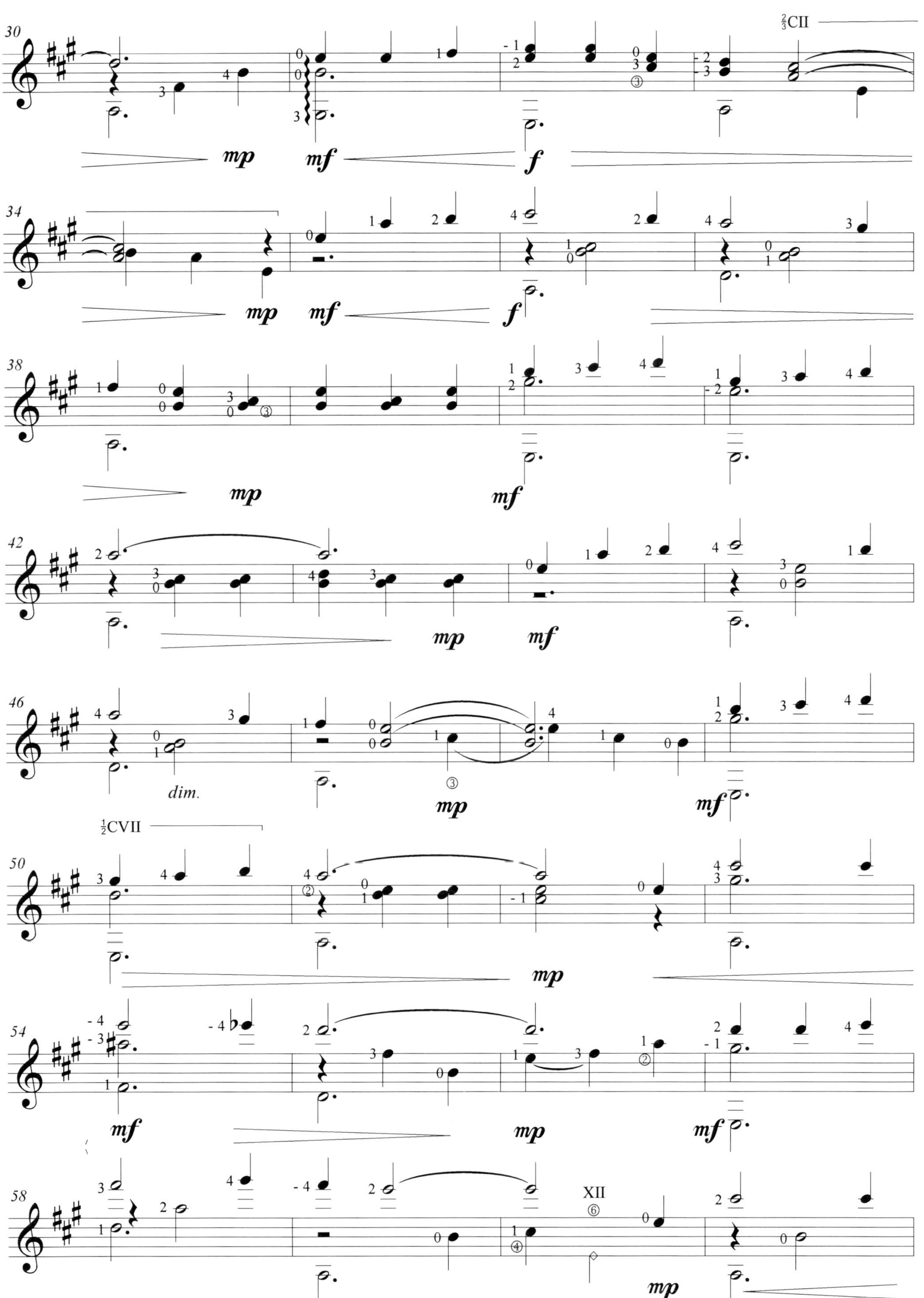

⅔CII
½CVII
mp
mf
f
dim.
XII

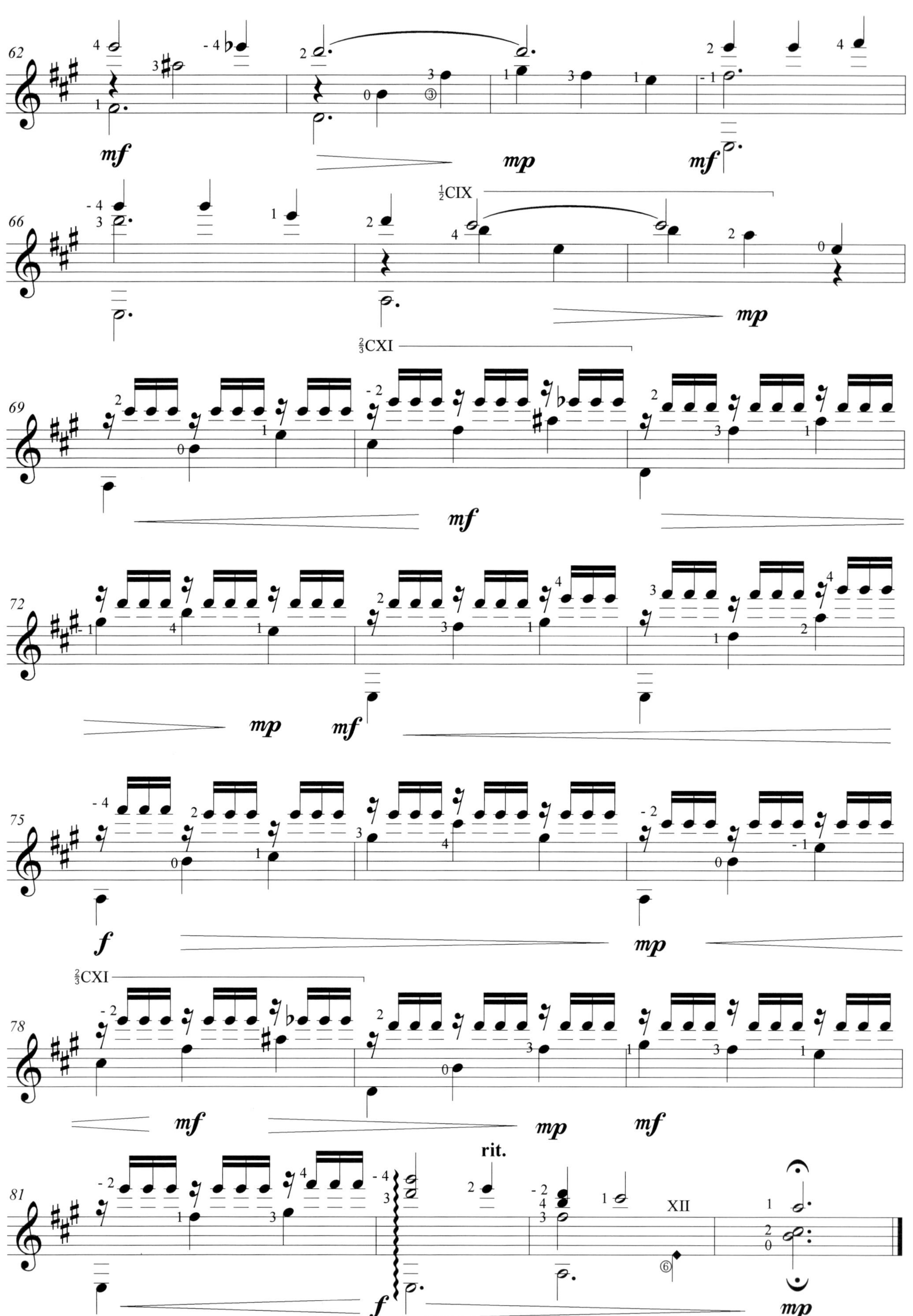
½CIX
⅔CXI
⅔CXI
rit.
XII
mf
mp
f

Other Mel Bay Classical Guitar Solo Books

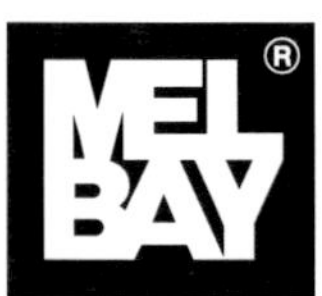